IMPOSSIBLE UNTIL DONE

ALFONSO AGUIRRE

¡Hi mom! ¡Hi dad! I dedicate this book to you.

I also dedicate this book to all the people determined to make this world a better place.

Contents

"It always seems impossible.

Until it's done."

–

Nelson Mandela

Author's Note

This book is me and the things that have been in my head for years.

And it's all about what happened during the time I was a college student.

Since the beginning, I felt there was a lot to do and that no one else was doing. I couldn't just focus on classes, doing homework, and studying for my exams. I would've gone crazy. Instead of that, I got involved into as much as I could. Because I believe we're in the world, not to think of it as it is, but to build it as it should be.

The world I imagine is way more united. Without division. Without fear. And the best thing we can do at this moment, is listen and know each other. This is my try to tell, in a very personal way, how things really are in Mexico. And what someone my age thinks we can to do change things.

The day I started writing this book, I looked for a journal that has been with me for more than six years. It has a black leather cover and cream color sheets. I don't just write anything that comes to my mind, if I did it would've been full a long time ago. It's just for special ideas. I used the first sheet when I was in the first semester in college. I wrote there the speech I would give to other students from different majors that were interested on creating a new student group of young people. We were ready to change and make things we believed in happen.

That student group was the most important thing I had done in my life until then. I was 100% sure that someone who was 19 years old could change the world. And I'm still sure.

But let's be honest. Making a change is hard. In school, in the government and even in companies. But fighting for something you believe in, will always be worth it. And all the amazing things that have happened in the world and in our own lives, at first, have seemed impossible. Until they were done.

This book is full of those stories, mine, and from people that I admire.

It's also about all those things I never imagined that would happen. Like enrolling on the last minute to an international summer that would change my life forever, and where I would meet women and men who would give me a new and different perspective of everything someone can do to actually change the world.

I didn't forget about the hard days. Like when I decided to switch my major five semesters after, while I was getting into my full-time job. And I also try to explain how it was to be the youngest, the only millennial, in a team full of seniors, that was in charge of a whole city.

Sometimes I didn't know where to get energy and time from. And it was normal to feel stressed. Sometimes I watched movies or series with characters who could solve a world crisis by working hard and intensely. I wanted to be like them. But while trying to do it, I stressed more and did less. And I ended up being the opposite of who I wanted to be.

Between so many things I wanted to do, the hours in the

day simply weren't enough to finish them. The one that suffered was my poor stomach.

And it was my fault to be so full of projects sometimes, and that I had to make the decision to quit some of them.

In my last six months as a student, after a big failure, I could find the time to calm myself. I also went to my first yoga classes, and even though I was sore for the first week, I discovered a way to connect with what really matters to me. Almost at the same time, I found a new quote to make things I planned happen: "Done is better than perfect". And step by step, I learned that I had to find a balance between who I am, what I like, and what I want to do.

They call it finding your purpose. Once you find it, you can easily set your priorities.

And I know not everyone likes talking about politics. I get why it's one of the forbidden topics when you have a family dinner. When you start the discussion, it has no end. Besides, most Mexicans are disappointed with all that has to do with political parties. I feel that way too. But not getting involved in politics is exactly what has brought us here.

Take this book as a different way to see things.

If you could run for public office, that would be great. We need decent people discussing and fixing the problems the whole world is facing. But if politics is not your thing, don't worry. It would be really boring to talk only about that. As you read along, you will know what a young person, or not so young, can do to build the world we all imagine living in. Also, you will find how to discover your purpose, make the most out of your potential and how to find new ideas and make them happen.

While all this happened, they told me that, one way or another, I like to get in trouble. Now that I think about it, I declare myself guilty. Every decision and project had its costs and sacrifices of every kind. Of course, it would've been easier and way more comfortable to just do my thing. But it would be very selfish. That's not what my country or the world need.

If getting in trouble is the only way to make a change, then you can count on me. And I hope that in the end I can count on you too.

IMPOSSIBLE
UNTIL DONE

NEW
BEGININGS

"Always deliver more than expected."

–

Larry Page

Next President

The president for the next six years is now in office.

One of the most important things in a democracy is the diversity of ideas and respect for different ways of thinking. So I can say without any problem that I didn't vote for him. I really don't understand the president's way of thinking or acting. But I wish with all my heart that someday, while I read the news, I will see that he and his government are doing well.

If his administration does well, it means that my country and every one of us, will do well too. I also wish that those who are part of his team and his political party listen to those who have a different vision to what might be the solutions that our country desperately needs. As Octavio Paz, one of the most recognized Latin American poets once said: "the greatest things we have done, were born from dialogue".

The world is full of doubts concerning the Mexican future. Still today no one can predict how López Obrador is going to react to each one of the problems our country is facing or predict the outcome of his actions in the coming years.

For reasons, that you might or might not know, we can't really be sure if the president will be consistent with his campaign promises and to the speech he has been giving for years. Or if he will change his mind every time that things don't seem convenient anymore for him or his team.

For more than 18 years I've been listening how many people thought he would be once in office. If you have heard what happened in Venezuela, well, people said that the same would happen to Mexico if Andrés Manuel won the election. That Mexico would become a dictatorship. Also, during the last campaign there were rumors that he was against all business owners, that he would stop all foreign investment coming to our country, that he would shut down hundreds of important factories and companies, that he would shut down legal reforms, and so on. Basically, that we were going to go backwards as a nation.

After all those rumors, no one knew what would happen or what to expect the night that he won the election. There was a general shock. And at least, when he was declared the winner, he tried to makes us feel calm. After the concession speech of each one of the other candidates, Andrés Manuel sent this message in his first speech as president elect:

"This new nation project will seek to establish an authentic democracy. We aren't betting on building either an open or undercover dictatorship", he said. He then added that the changes he will make will be deep, but always sticking to the law.

There are many challenges to face in those changes that our country needs.

Almost half of the Mexican population are living in poverty. You may have heard that there are huge cases of corruption practices on a daily basis. We don't have the economic growth we should have. We have the worst educational indexes on an international level. And the list goes on and on. I bet you can complete it.

But of course, there's a solution to each and every single one of this problems. And just now, the hope for a change is much bigger than before. In all of Mexico's history, it had never happened that a presidential candidate would win with more than 50% of the votes.

And we have to be careful with hope being placed in only one person. Not everything depends on the President. After all, we're a democracy with balance of power. There's the executive one, the legislative, and the judicial one. A President doesn't have, and he shouldn't have, all the power. But Lopez Obrador's party has won the majority of the spots in Congress and they were sworn in one month before him. In theory the legislative power is independent from the executive one. If the President sends an initiative to the Congress, it should be evaluated and voted independently from each deputy's and senator's political affiliation. But we have seen how things work in Mexico. They don't work as they should. I'm worried that Lopez Obrador could send an initiative to Congress and that it is immediately approved. Without a critical nor a serious analysis.

If we keep letting them do what they want, this won't change. And it's simpler than it seems. People from government are your representatives. But if they don't know what you want, and they know you're not keeping an eye in them, they are in total liberty.

It's not a secret that people of all ages are disappointed and completely done with political parties. It's even not well seen to be part of them. And being part of the government is even worse seen. Maybe, we were hoping that with the rejection we have given to politicians, they would react to our apathy and distrust. We think that, if they saw us angry and with no intention to support them, they would renovate to correct their ills. But the opposite happened. It seems that they make worse decisions each time. And every time we think that they can't disappoint us even more, they surprise us again.

Even so, we the citizens haven't had the courage to be part of a non-governmental organization. Nor to link universities with the private sector. Or even bette, to choose a cause and fight for it. Something that would've been normal if we would have wanted to get rid of political parties once and for all.

What we do is criticize any mistake and anyone who attempts to do something. This is important: the country's not going to change with our opinion. Much more than that is needed. Above all, action.

And seek an organized change.

We have the potential. In Mexico, contrary to many other first world countries, the youth is a majority. It's incredible. Because is European and many Asian countries people are choosing not to have kids.

But this proportion of a youth majority comes with an enormous responsibility. And the reality is that our entire generation has different ideas for the country. And they are really great. The problem is that they're just staying as ideas.

This is the perfect moment to make those ideas happen. The biggest challenge, right now, for all Mexicans and every citizen of the world, is to take action. Everywhere I go there are signs of hope. But we have to go further. We have to get fully involved.

The election day I participated watching over a polling place. I wanted to make sure that the people's votes would be respected there. They told me that in the neighborhood where that polling place was, it was normal for groups from one political party to cheat. And to try to change the outcome during the counting of the votes. That's why I never took an eye off the polling place. And I never lost sight of the ballot box where people would place their votes.

For the ten hours I spent there, nothing alarming or strange happened.

Up until night time.

It became really complicated to count the votes. There were more than 20 possible combinations, because there were some kind of political alliances. But we did everything very carefully. The PRI had always won at that polling place, it turned out Lopez Obrador had won. And as I kept counting votes, I got the "Uno Noticias" notification on my phone. I never subscribed to that service, like many, but at least that day it was useful. It said José Antonio Meade and Ricardo Anaya had gone out to accept their defeat.

A year before I had witnessed the election for Governor in Coahuila, my state. What happened was that two candidates declared themselves the winner just at the same time. And both assured to have the certificates that proved it. The story didn't end until the discussion went to court five months later. That wasn't good for the state and its citizens. A lot of political and economical uncertainty was generated. Many investments didn't arrive because of that.

And those were months wasted that could've been used on an ordered transition of power. And time that could've been used to plan how the next government would be.

At a national level, it also happened in 2008 with president Felipe Calderon's election and the great march that López Obrador organized. He even made up his own Inauguration Day. Fake. Invented. And out of the law. But he said he was the legitimate president. And I imagined something like that would happen again this time. The whole presidential election ending up in the Supreme Court. The candidates between accusations of stealing votes. News of how they manipulated the counting systems. And all the things we always hear about.

But it was different this time. There was none of that.

Even that same night when the election was over, the president Enrique Peña Nieto sent a message to the nation recognizing Lopez Obrador's triumph. He called out for a peaceful and lawful transition of power. Two days later, they had their first meeting in the National Palace. Those kinds of actions send a message: that there's a democratic continuity in our government. And that we have a modern electoral system. The result was that the Mexican peso appreciated the next day. And the political uncertainty of our country decreased.

But when things flow this way, there's also the one who thinks everything was settled way before. "That's why they accept defeat so fast". "The President had everything settled". I have friends who always imagine the worst out of everything. I call them the conspiracists. Under their eyes everything that happens in the country, or even in the world, was previously settled or planned. Even the smallest detail.

Well, I don't believe it. What I do believe is that things are way simpler than they sometimes seem. And that we, as citizens, can change the course of what happens.

This idea that everything was settled intensified in august, two months after the elections, when López Obrador and José Antonio Meade met. Again, there were those who started to accuse that everything was already settled. And that the PRI had helped Morena win. I liked how León Krauze expressed it in a tweet:

"Let's take it down a notch. There's
nothing perverse or a sign of any collusion
in the meeting between López Obrador
and Meade. It's what happens, ideally, in a
civilized democracy between the winner
and the candidate who recognizes and
assumes his defeat. That's how it should
always occur (and should have occurred
before)".

I completely agreed with him. There are many things done in modern and advanced democracies that we're not used to in Mexico. Like Krauze says, that's how it should have always been.

The reason why López Obrador won is very clear to us. I think we all know. There was anger towards the mayor political parties for not having delivered the results they promised. There was progress with both, yes. But the expectations from Mexicans aren't low anymore. And even though they say as an excuse that in six or twelve years a change can't be made, there are countries that have done it.

We have to be very attentive to what happens in these coming years. We owe López Obrador and Morena an open mind and an opportunity. But change should never be about only one election or one single person. We live in a democracy, after all. That's why we, besides an open mind, also owe the country a more active participation than ever before. All the time. For real.

Several years ago, Manuel, my best friend and I, partnered to make the company we always wanted to have. We help companies and people innovate in marketing, logistics, and communications. Like anyone who loves those topics, both of us, besides business, are passionate about campaigns. Including political campaigns (when they're well made).

We were really excited by the beginning of 2018. There would be local and national elections in our country. We were eager to see everything the candidates would do. But we were also desperate to be part of one of their teams and help the best profile win.

Without knowing what and how, we got a golden ticket opportunity.

Something happened when the former first lady ran for president. Margarita Zavala began collecting signatures to become an independent candidate. And we were given the news that her team would meet us. They ask us for a proposal for their digital campaign strategy.

We were preparing really well for that presentation. Without sleeping for several days, we did the homework. We researched and studied what presidential candidates like Barack Obama in his 2008 and 2012 campaigns. And we look also for other examples. Hillary Clinton in 2016. And Emmanuel Macron in 2017. All of them had achieved to build the most innovative campaigns in history.

But, in Mexico, the normal thing is to do the kind of campaign that everyone is used to. And that no one likes. They're always something like this: two or three months with tv and radio ads. Posting events on Facebook and Twitter. And announcing very similar promises and issues to the rest of the candidates. They all promise more safety. More jobs. Less poverty. Oh man, such geniuses.

What they have done in other countries is demonstrate they want to win. How? By making the best effort. Reuniting the best team. Recruiting experts in each topic. Building the best campaign. And engaging the most number of citizens in it.

In the documentary called "Mitt" done by Netflix, we can see how the day of a presidential candidate is like. It's a behind the scenes about governor Mitt Romney's campaign during his campaign against Barack Obama.

There was a scene that which caught my attention the most. While the team was preparing a video production of one of their promotional videos, someone from the team said: "In a presidential campaign, everything has to be and look perfect. If something goes wrong, you're suggesting that how his government might be".

And there's a clear and direct message that I want to send to all the presidential candidates we had in 2018. Margarita, Ricardo, Andrés, José y Jaime: you didn't meet the expectations. Neither of you did. Your campaigns didn't give the image of being perfect. Actually all the contrary. All of them were full of mistakes. But you didn't learn from them. And someone's campaign reflects a lot how that person is. And the government they might have.

I followed them all on Twitter. And every time I saw one of their videos, I imagined their presidency or the government they would have. Andrés López Obrador's with incomplete ideas and with a team coming out to explain what he tried to say, generating more confusion and panic. With big crowd events and media that wouldn't question him. Ricardo Anaya's generating a great expectation only to let us down later, with a fragmented team and stuck the same media scandal for all six years, dragging him to take mediocre actions and ending up with an unplanned government. Rather improvised. Jose Antonio Meade's, a continuation from Enrique Peña Nieto's government. With a team full of recognized characters from our country's political history, but few experts on the urgent topics to solve. Except for him, recognized as an intellectual. But of course, with a whole structure saying that Mexico is the number one country and that everything's fine.

During the three unbearable months of campaigns, I didn't see a single article on any newspaper or magazine talking about innovation or any of the five campaigns.

What was I expecting? At least, what we had seen in other countries: a team of experts in data analytics and micro targeting to get to potential voters. A team deeply researching the country's problems and testing with numbers to see different scenarios and verify the viability of the solutions their candidate was presenting. A team of experts in digital and on-site organization, recruiting volunteers and leading thousands of actions across the country. A team of marketers trying with different messages, colors and slogans. A team dedicated to writing the speeches. A digital innovation team to get to every platform in a striking way. Not just posting events. Everything, under the vision and direction of a CEO. A planning expert campaign coordinator. That's how this century's campaigns are like. As if they were a startup. But because as we saw, not yet in Mexico.

When I get myself reflecting about it I don't understand why the five candidates never took the time to google "How did Obama win?". It would've been enough if they had seen the first five search results so they could get an idea of what they had to do.

The first time that Barack Obama ran for president I was in secondary school, and I perfectly remember that everyone and all the media were talking about how he revolutionized political campaigns because he was the first candidate to make the most out of social media. That was in 2008. And four years later, in his reelection campaign in 2012, he innovated again by creating an internet platform that organized his volunteers across the country. And we have to add his great talent for public speaking and the great charisma he has. He was also one of the first authentic politicians who opened up. He was never afraid of showing his emotions, what he felts and thought. He laughed and joked in his speeches. In others he confessed anger or disappointment. In others he sang and in others he cried. In the end, a candidate or a president, they are people too. Not robots.

Two years before our campaigns, the world was paying attention to two very important ones: the election for President of the United States and the one for President of France. At least I was excessively watching them.

In 2016 Hillary Clinton gathered the best team. Half of them were ex White House workers who resigned to work with her. The second half of her team were recognized professionals from Silicon Valley companies. And thousands of them were volunteers. She had two campaign directors. One was an expert in politics and traditional campaigns, and the other one was very young and an expert in campaigns and modern strategies. They made amazing things in branding and marketing. Also in politics and organization. In the end she raised more than 3 billion dollars with donations from millions of people. And they achieved to connect a whole volunteer base with an app. She didn't win. But she got almost 3 million votes more than Donald Trump. Even though she didn't get to be the first woman President of the United States, the experts acknowledge she made one of the best campaigns.

And in 2017, the campaign that Emmanuel Macron made, took the best out of other candidates around the world and improved it. He started a movement called *En Marche!*, to which many volunteers signed in. As part of his strategy, the campaigned achieved to create algorithms, along with a company dedicated to digital topics, to identify the districts and neighborhoods where there was the possibility that they would vote for Macron, thanks to data they had gathered from their app. They recruited thousands of volunteers digitally. And volunteers not only handed out flyers. The campaign organized them to go knock on doors of more potential voters. They knocked more than 300,000 doors in total. And they had more than 25,000 interviews to feed the campaign's data base on problems and topics that interested people. That helped build the proposals and policies that they would later implement as a government. That's what I never heard about in Mexico during this past election. To me, that's demonstrating you want to win. That's demonstrating you will make a government with everyone's help.

I thought that at least one or two candidates in Mexico would do that. Especially, the younger ones. But none of them did. And part of the problem why we hate campaigns is that we don't feel part of them. Because they haven't tried to do it.

When Manuel and I got off the plane, in Mexico City's airport, I turned off my phone's airplane mode. I looked for the contact of who was going to meet us to let them know we had already arrived. Several minutes later I saw the WhatsApp notification with the reply: there was a change in the schedule. They would meet us a bit later. Luckily, we had bought the return ticket later that day. And with that change we would have one or two hours to rest a little. We hadn't had any sleep. We spent all night making the last changes to the presentation and we went to the airport very early in the morning to take the first flight of the day. Without any sleep.

Actually, we couldn't believe it. We were about to get to the campaign headquarters of the first woman in Mexico who was seeking her independent candidacy to the presidency. On top of that, that day, October 17th, it was the celebration of the 64th anniversary when the women's right to vote was recognized. To commemorate it, we were about to put in our best effort to get to support one of them become President. It was the perfect day. What can I say? I love supporting women.

We arrived. And the person who was going to meet us notified us of other last minute change in the schedule. So he asked one of his team members to meet us and hear what he had to present. Like Emmanuel Macron's style, we took the best from other campaigns and improved it. We gave our best ideas and our plan.

Sometimes one recognizes when a battle is lost. That's how we felt when we realized the person we were presenting to, wasn't so attracted by our ideas. In fact, in the end he even made us the comment "we don't need so much marketing". Still today I ask myself how a campaign wouldn't need it.

As soon as we got out of the campaign headquarters, we looked at each other. And without saying anything both of us saw in the other a face of disappointment. The campaign had a big problem. We went to the airport and went back to our city. Without understanding how they weren't interested on building and having an innovative campaign.

That same day in the afternoon, we saw Margarita posted a photo in which she appeared, far away, celebrating the anniversary to women's voting in Mexico sitting in a Starbucks, with one or two people gathering signatures. Not one speech. Not one exciting video. Nor an inspiring quote.

We get it. The process of gathering all those citizens' signatures was extremely exhausting. It's definitely almost impossible getting to be an independent candidate in Mexico. But we're in the era of making the impossible, possible. And she did achieve to gather the signatures. She got to be candidate. When that happened, there was still some hope in us that they would be interested on making a campaign like Macron's or Obama's. Trust me, we tried. We sent them all our presentations with ideas and examples. We knew they had economical problems. But the point was to make history. We were so desperate to see an amazing campaign in Mexico, that we even offered them the whole strategy and execution from our company for free. Our insistence was because it was a historic moment for Mexico. That deserved the most innovative campaign. One that would inspire millions of women, young people, and children. But the team ended up really tired and exhausted with the signature collection, just as they confessed it themselves.

We know what happened later. A campaign that never ignited. And that one day surprised us with her resignation. Something that everyone applauded. The resignation with which we heard the real Margarita talk about her values, what she felt, the problems she saw. It was the most authentic version of her we have seen. But there's something here that gets my attention.

The speech that Hillary Clinton gave when she lost and recognized her defeat in the 2016 sections was catalogued as the best one she has given. They said she was authentic, emotive, strong, respectful, visionary, and inspiring. Exactly what they told Margarita Zavala when she quit.

Jennifer Palmieri, former communications director from Hillary's campaign, in her most recent book, claims that we like those moments because in our (primitive) subconscious, that's what we think a woman should do. Putting others' interests before their own. Grant. Accept the defeat. Let someone else take control. It's something to reflect two or three times. Perhaps we're losing many big opportunities in the county's public life, in companies, and in organizations because we're paying attention to that subconscious we have.

I hope one day I can see a woman President in Mexico. And I want to be there to support her doing my part so she wins. I also hope one day I can see a campaign that will move us. That inspires us. That organizes us. An innovative campaign. Mexico needs it more than ever.

I'll never be able to forget how the debates were before. In 2012, when Josefina Vázquez Mota, Enrique Peña Nieto, Gabriel Quadri, or Andrés Manuel López Obrador spoke, it seemed as is each one of them was in a different place. They didn't answer They didn't answer each other and never exchanged a look.

The moderator only said two kind of things. "Time's over" and "The next question is..." and he randomly pulled it from an urn. Later on, the candidates didn't answer and they talked about what they wanted. The moderator never intervened. He didn't moderate. Those were not debates. Those were exhibitions.

Many, or most of the debates with candidates for mayor, governor, deputies or senators are like that. With generic questions. And without the moderator's intervention. In fact, many arrive at the debate and they even have to read what they say. I have this personal policy: if I see a candidate reading at a debate, it gets dismissed within my possibilities. Because they didn't prepare. And if they were like that for a debate, they will be like that in their government.

Now I was expecting some action. But I didn't see it coming. I thought they would be the same as before. I was literally left mouth open from surprise by the first minutes of the first debate the Electoral Institute organized in this last election. It was almost instantaneously that I could realize they had modernized themselves. Even in the smallest details. The Palace of Mining in Mexico City looked amazing. Even the lighting was modern.

And the best of all: the dynamic.

It began quickly. Straight to the point. The moderators were making questions that every candidate was worthy of. If there was a personal scandal, they asked them about that. If there was a confusing topic, they asked them about that. If they wandered from the topic, they interrupted them to get them back to the question. The times were distributed in a way that the debate was dynamic. If one of them questioned another one, they made sure the question wasn't left up in the air. That was a real debate. And that wasn't it! Each one of the three debates had different formats.

Mi total recognition goes to those who organized it this way. I felt proud that at least the National Electoral Institute was modernizing itself. The fact that they were analyzing how things are in other countries. The next step at the national level is making the debates pat of the most important moments of an election.

And if in the next debate you see, in any type of election, you see that one of the candidates questions another one, don't see it as something bad or as an attack. We have the right to know the truth and to them clarifying the topics in which there's confusion. Don't count how many proposals each of them made, either. In the end, it's a debate. Not a proposal exhibition. Instead, we can look at how they react to the questionings. How much did they prepare. Why are they running. What differentiates them from the other candidates. How do they face truths or lies. How do they think. How do they treat others. How fo they act under pressure. What arguments and proof do they have that their proposals are what the country needs. All of that is important in a President. In fact, it's important in every public office.

Presenting proposals is basic. But that's what the speeches they give, their websites, and their books (they will do it if they're someone who's making the effort to make their ideas known) are for. And in this past election I didn't see a big effort to communicate them.

Ricardo Anaya mentioned a book in the first debate which contained his proposals and his government plan. But later on, his team went out to clarify that the book wasn't available to the public. How many bizarre things happened in the campaigns! Just like when José Antonio Meade didn't remember the name of his own book. Margarita Zavala and Andrés Manuel López Obrador had already published one with their visions for the country before the campaigns started.

I was bothered every time I visited the website of one of them. They did publish their proposals. But there are ways. What they did was copy paste the text in their website. They even appeared with a small size. Without spaces between lines. Without highlighted quotes. Without colors. And I know why they did it like that. Because they weren't interested in people reading them. When that interests you, you think how can you do it so that each one of your proposals is understood and communicated the best way possible.

I'm no longer going to mention names or places (you can already imagine who I'm referring to), but this is a great example: in another country a candidate (a woman) had a proposal to reduce the enormous credits people pay to go to college. To make the proposal understandable, attractive, and more illustrative, this person put up in her website a proposal simulation. Any user could get in, choose of how many years the credit was. The amount of money they owed. Their ages. And some other questions and data. In the end, the website put up a customized comparison with what they paid now for their credits, against what they could pay and in how much time, if the candidate's proposal became reality.

She did that with many of her proposals. Look for innovative ways to explain how they would work. That's demonstrating you want to win, and that you want those who could vote for you to understand to perfection each one of your proposals.

It was hard to choose who to vote for. I hate, like many, have to choose the least worst.

That's going to end when we decide to actively participate in the country's decisions. When we demand. When we march. When we organize (what I talk about somewhere in this book). And, mostly, when everyone is open to run for public office. You don't have to run to be president from one day to another. You can start being your neighborhood's president. Or your career's president at your university. President of the parent's association at your kids' school. Or president of a businessmen's group. We need the right people at the right public offices.

When you do it, give your best effort. Your work and performance don't have to be perfect. Just be brave. Kind. And resilient. That day will be incredible. It's not going to be about choosing the least worst. It's going to be about a hard decision to choose the best. But what do you do when it's not like that yet?

Spoiling the vote is something I've always been against. I do think it's a way to complain that none of the options represent you, and a way to demand that there's netter candidates next time. I considered it many times this last time. Choosing someone was more important than making a complaint. Because even if I spoilt it or not, someone was going to win. And that person wasn't going to reflect about the amount of spoilt votes. In fact, it's something those who didn't win should ask themselves. Waiting to make a whole auto analysis on why they lost.

I wanted to define my vote during the last days of campaign. I was awaiting some candidate prepared to be President. During the campaigns everything had happened. But it was now the time for them to give the closure and ask the Mexicans' vote one last time. I imagined them preparing and writing the best speech of their lives. Different drafts and hundreds of corrections. In my head I imagined them rehearsing for those last days. Each of their teams, organizing the last event with perfect logistics. With stages where the candidate would go up. Just them standing in front of a presidential podium. Giving the message that would convince us all. A speech to prove their experience and capacity to govern.

During the three months of campaign none of them behaved that way. But in the end, I was sure it will be like that. In the end, they were running to become President of Mexico. At some moment, sooner or later, they had to demonstrate what they could be.

What I saw, instead, were videos of the candidates dancing. Taking the mic to say anything that would come up in the moment. And shouting chanting slogans in poorly organized events.

That disappoints me. "That's how campaigns are in Mexico", they tell me very often. Well yes. That's how they are. But it doesn't mean they have to keep being like that.

In the end, López Obrador won.

We can't know who will be the president in 2024, in 2030, or in 2036. But there's on a small probability that this person is reading this book. Maybe it's even you. Maybe you're still a student, or a business woman, or a teacher or a woman entrepreneur. Maybe you're a man or a woman. Maybe you're already in the public life, or not yet and you see it as something totally external to you. Maybe you already decided you want to become President or maybe you don't know it yet and you imagine a completely different future for you. But you have to take this into account: it's worth it. It's completely worth it.

You also need to know that if you want to win, if you really wish to make a change in the country, if you believe in your capacity to solve problems and get us on the right track, you have to demonstrate it. And the best way to demonstrate it is to make a campaign at the level of the office you're looking to get into. Seeking the presidency is seeking to occupy the most important office in the country. We have to give it the importance it deserves. We do need to realize it is our greatest representative. The President doesn't do it alone. They can't do it alone. But a President makes decisions and defines actions and the agenda during 6 years.

In a country like Mexico, where there's very low participation from people or NGOs and in which the participation from the private sector in public topics is a challenge, the elections should be more important.

The life expectancy in Mexico is 76 years. In an entire lifetime, a Mexican is going to see 12 Presidents. Only 12. And given that we can vote until 18, someone will only have the chance to choose 9. So we can't afford play with one of those nine decisions we will have to make in our life.

I already voted in two. I have seven left. In those seven elections, I will be demanding that the candidates are the best profiles. And that they make campaigns that will sum as all.

"If you want to be somebody, somebody really special, be yourself."

\-

Anonymous

Change of Plans

Summer vacations ended in August. And the last semester of my career started. The first days of class everyone was still talking about how López Obrador had won. And what were we expecting to happen when he was sworn in. But something was for sure, we had to keep making the effort to be the best students so later we could be the best professionals. There was nothing more. The country had already decided. So I tried not to worry a lot about that.

After spending more time studying than I expected, it was only the one last effort I had left. And I wanted to be totally focused in making the most out of my last classes and my last days in university. Just like almost all my classmates, I had small crisis in which I didn't know what I was going to do from now on. There were only some months left for my graduation. The entry to the real world. But I set myself to take those last months to be calm. I had spent many years running from one place to another.

I still perfectly remember how I chose my career when I was about to graduate from High School. It occurred to me to open YouTube to look for ideas. Among many things that I liked, it was hard to decide what was I going to dedicate to for life. You know the video thing is. You see one that takes you to another. When you realize it's been hours. From video to video, I got to one that explained all the engineering work that's behind the Disney themed parks. Mostly, the one in Orlando. The daily logistics. The imagination team that planned the new attractions. The innovation they put into each of their parks. Pure perfection! There's a reason why we say it's the happiest place on Earth. That video interviewing all the team members inspired me to do the same. The next day I ran to enroll to the Industrial and Systems Engineering career.

Getting into the university was something really exciting. And somewhat intimidating. I felt I didn't know anything in comparison to all my classmates who knew everything. Almost six months had to go by for me to gets used to and realize that in fact, we all were under the same conditions. It was a matter of gaining confidence.

I liked the classes. Mostly the ones that were like "Economy for the creation of companies" or "Analysis and Verbal Expression". The ones other engineering students called fillers or common part. It was very evident to see the things that caught my attention and those that didn't. And it was noticeable that every new semester my friends told me that career wasn't for me. I don't know if because of being stubborn or optimistic, I convinced myself, and according to me I also convinced others, that it was the perfect career for me. But it wasn't.

We're imperfect. If we weren't, it would be really boring. And not very authentic. But I didn't know it then. I clung to the plan. I knew I wasn't going to dedicate myself to the industry when I graduated. And without realizing it I was going through what us millennials try to avoid at all costs: stand something you don't like to do, where you don't see a purpose, and something you think is going to take you nowhere.

It wasn't months. It was semesters without making the most out of my potential. In classes. Because there was nothing to say about extracurricular activities. Every time my parents saw me arriving at midnight, they just asked "now what did you enroll in?".

I liked to participate. I even made my own student group. It was called "Voz Joven".

The 2012 presidential elections had just passed and I felt the desire to make a change all the time. In fact, the original idea for Voz Joven was for it to be a political student group that promoted initiatives and to make the youngest ones have a place to discuss and debate ideas. And make them happen. Our phrase or slogan was going to be "the best place for youth is politics".

When we got to register the group to the Tec, they told us that, according to the regulations, those types of groups couldn't be registered, the ones that ha political topics. We had to change the whole concept. And all the planning we had. Now, some years later, the Tec allows and even encourages not only for its students to form student group with political topics. But also encourage that students organize themselves around topics like human rights and the LGBT rights agenda.

We changed everything, and it turned out to be better. We could be dedicated to political matters, but we promoted culture instead. Reading in kids. Recycling. We made awareness and reflexion events. And, mostly, we made students participate more. Because once they were in Voz Joven and they became part of something, when they were done, they looked for another activity in other group. Goal reached.

There were things that went wrong. Like when we sent a letter by mail to all the deputies and senators of the country to confirm their attendance to an event called Cultural Reform. We wanted to send the message that law reforms weren't very important if we didn't change our habits and our lack of participation. Things like being on time. Comply. Plan. And all of that. Due to the fact that none of the deputies nor senators confirmed their attendance, we canceled the event.

There were also things that went better than we thought they would. Like an event we made called Talents' Night. We wanted to exhibit all the hidden talents from the high school and college students. Whatever they were.

It was our first event. We didn't know how hard it was to sell tickets. To get sponsorships. And mostly to get people to be interested. We didn't know what to do on the day of the event. Everything went way better than we imagined. And more than six hundred people came. Of course we organized it again the following year. And the public grew to more than nine hundred. That day selfies had become famous thanks to Ellen DeGeneres in the Oscars. At our event, Roger González, the guest host, took one with all the audience. It was the new thing. And you can see how all the nine hundred people were euphoric to be in it.

All those events required the most part of my time. Not just to organize them. The best team had to be recruited. Write letters. Send emails. Make calls. Plan logistics. Design advertisement. Ask for sponsorships. And solve thousands of problems. I grew as a person and as a professional thanks to all of that.

But you can't do everything at the same time. One day, people from my "Physics II" class and the ones from "Electricity and Magnetism", sent a photo to the group we had in WhatsApp in which I was at an interview in the CNN program "Mexico Opina" talking about the structural reforms to our law that Enrique Peña Nieto was proposing. Back then they weren't approved yet. But they were about to be. And my friends were laughing because they said it was easier to see me on the CNN channel than in the classroom.

And I was like that for several semesters, organizing and looking for activities that would fill me. Because the Industrial Engineering career didn't do it.

One weekend I finished reading "Why nations fail?" almost at the same time that I read "Hard Choices". Both talked about the problems the world is now facing. "If I keep reading books and articles about all this, I want to dedicate myself to it!", I thought. I perfectly remember it was a Sunday. Like if I needed another signal from heaven to realize things, Hillary Clinton published a video announcing she was going to run for the Presidency. Well, I also had to start making my own choices. Hard choices. On Monday (the next day) I was already at my university's offices starting the paperwork to switch careers.

I don't regret the time I lost. But I wish I had listened to my friends and professors before. The bright side: I know more things about engineering than any other International Business graduate. On top of that, I love the career I chose. It's very specific in the topics we covered, but at the same time very open, given the fact that it's about a whole world.

My favorite classes were the ones where we studied countries' cultures and how each one of them has different ways of making things happen. I also loved to simulate negotiations or solve some company's problem with a new strategy.

It was the best decision I could have made. And when I switched careers I still wanted to keep doing a lot of things. I don't know where I got so much energy. I wanted to start a business. Change the world. Be successful. But I knew that, as they say, first things first. That career switch came with another important decision. From now on I was going to pay for my career.

That's how I got to my first job (the first formal one). For the first time, I split my time in only two things: school and work. I was going to miss everything I did in the student groups. But I had to learn to focus and dedicate all of my energy to my two priorities.

That first job was in my city's local government. The Mayor back then was Isidro López. At first, I was in his wife's team, or "tía Lourdes", how I call her. After some time, we began to see more people started to follow her, and the team liked how she started to improve her communication strategy. That's why they decided to move me to the Mayor's team, to make him have an excellent digital strategy as well.

I loved working for them. And it was there, where I learned the most.

Now it's easier than before to observe what a politic does. But with the experience I got, I can assure you there are more things than you can imagine behind a government. Things you don't see in the Facebook or Twitter profiles. I was living all of that for several years, without the filter of media. Living it personally.

My role there wasn't defined at all (and I didn't want it to be). I got in to help, mostly, in communication topics. But I could be an executive assistant. Write speeches. Plan strategies. Give opinions on projects. Tweet. Produce videos. And in the end I even spent several days without sleeping fixing the last government report because they hired a company that didn't know how to do it.

There's a really big amount of things they don't teach us in school. And those things seem normal when you're working. It's not a grade with just an evaluation form anymore. Everything counts. It's not studying for the text anymore. It's demonstrating your capacity to do things and solve problems every minute you're there. It's not semesters, classes, tests, or homework anymore. It's real life.

I wasn't easy. It was very exhausting. And even with all that work, homework and school projects, every time I saw an important meeting in the Mayor's schedule about topics that interested me, like transport, security, or about new projects to solve my city's problems, I asked for permission to go. Even if it didn't have to do with my job. If there's someone reading this who could hack my phone, they would see the many messages I sent the Mayor and his wife asking them if I could get into a meeting about this or the other. Sometimes they were very serious topics. To get in, I promised them to sit in the farthest place and just listen without saying anything. The thing was to learn.

I tried many times to do more things at the same time on top of classes and work. Sometimes it worked. Sometimes it didn't. Every project requires time. You can't do everything in one day, like I thought before. That's why they rightly repeat us the phrase "jack of all trades, master of none".

I did stop organizing events and activities for student groups. There was no way for me to keep doing it. But work got me excited too. The moment I realized I was doing more than I was asked to do. I also stopped seeing my friends. Some of them I only saw in classes. A public apology for all those times I cancelled plans or didn't reply to messages. I ended up totally exhausted and the only thing I wanted to do when I had free time was to get into my room and read a good book. To relax and be able to truly disconnect, I did choose books that had absolutely nothing to do with politics, nor government, nor work culture, nor digital campaigns. Like "The Cuckoo's Calling" by Robert Galbraith (more known as J.K. Rowling), "The Pillars of the Earth" by Ken Follet (big enough to serve as a self defense weapon) and even "The Golden Compass" (from the list of forbidden books). I could set my mind in a different pace with that.

I couldn't stop being myself either. When there was time, I watched series like "House of Cards", "Designated Survivor", "Madame Secretary", and "Scandal", all of them, stories that happen in the White House. There are episodes in which there's characters who can solve a world crisis in five minutes and have everything under control. Those were my favorites. And my Safari's history is full of digital strategies, communication, and innovation articles from the best brands in the world and articles on public policies that have worked in other countries.

There were very tiring days when everything came

together. Classes in the morning. Meetings or work events at noon. Classes again in the afternoon. Sometimes events that finished last at night. And I had to wake up very early the next day. I survived those days with my green smoothies and my protein bars. Remembering my favorite characters from my books and series, and the people I admire in real life, it helped me to keep going. If they could do it, why not me?

I wasn't always healthy. We all in the team ate Rancheritos. The Mayor's wife told us she only ate that snack because a nutritionist told her they were made of nixtamalized corn and they were baked. Not fried in oil, like the others. It became word of mouth. So there was always a Rancheritos bag in all the meetings and all the vans. Until we realized, after years, that it was a lie. And they had more fat in them than others. And it was then that we stopped eating them (so often).

In my classes I didn't organize myself, but with a really demanding full time job I couldn't have the perfect grades I wanted. But I managed to do well. Up until that moment I had already done many extra things that compensated it. Like learn to lead teams. Organize the logistics of various events. And get big amounts of money with sponsorships to make them happen. And now this new job.

I was meeting a lot of people. And each day was completely different to the other. That's what I loved the most. There were no routines. The most exciting thing was that I could apply what I had been learning for years. I could make a change.

There were four things during that time that kept me proactive and energized. One: believing that with my job I could have an impact, as little as it was, in my city and my community. Two: having the certainty that the Mayor was an honest person who reminded us daily why we were there. Three: The affection and trust of his wife (she was the one who let me experiment new ideas and strategies). Four: I updated myself and learned what else could be done.

The money I earned went straight to my university, gas, food, and a lot of coffee. I had nothing left to save (and I still have debts). But I had decided to do that. I had to make the most out of the opportunity that all the circumstances and my effort were giving me. There're people who wanted to get into the same university as me and due to economic reasons they didn't. People who were looking for some job and didn't find it. And people trying to find something they liked and they couldn't discover what it was. I had the three things at the same time. Every time I remember that I feel very grateful. With life. With God. With my parents. With my grandparents. With my friends. And I wish that everyone could have the same opportunities as me, or better ones.

Any student in Mexico should feel free to be able to choose the career they like the most. In the university they're more passionate about. Without any worries. That working at the same time becomes an option. But also, if someone wants to dedicate to being a full-time student, that they don't have to worry about how they're going to pay their tuition either. That's the Mexico I believe we can have. For anyone.

Before, when I imagined a Mayor's office, a governor's or even the president's itself, I thought it was like a secret headquarter with monitors everywhere. Real time updated indicators. A wall sized map with red dots appearing and disappearing. The e-mail full of reports and summaries. Cameras from the city playing. Aerial views. And a team making decisions every minute.

The reality is very different. And it's not in real time. In the government things happen like in slow motion. Very slow. It seems contradictory, because there are many urgent topics.

One of my first frustrations: no one used e-mail. And that's even when it's something from fifteen or twenty years ago (I was born with an email account). Companies started a paper saving culture from the eighties. The US Congress even passed a bill in 2000 so electronically signed documents had legal validity.

When I tried to send one: No! It has to be in a printed document. Ah! With a letterhead. With a label. Printed and signed by hand with blue ink. With several copies for a file. And the signature of receiving can't be missed. Very outdated and slow for this time.

If the email isn't used, some portal or app for monitoring efficiency, diving tasks, sharing calendars are much less to be used. No Slack, Asana, Wunderlist, nor Trello. Less even Google Drive, iCloud or Dropbox. This is serious: in which era did the government get stuck into? When I talked about implementing something like that they just gave me a look. Like they didn't understand me.

I was used to, for any process in my university, just login online, look for the right section, and it's done. Everything automized. In the companies it's absolutely normal to use this kind of things. In fact, it's an enormous tendency. All of them make the information between collaborators flow and be almost instantaneous. They make the job faster and efficient. They improve in their internal processes, but they also improve in the customer service they give. The difference: those companies focus on clients. Governments are focused on other things which are clearly not us the citizens.

I know that many are going to keep with the same promises as always. But in the nest elections I'm going to look for and support the candidate that proposes to reinvent the government and make it a *Great Place to Work*. That's going to be a great difference. From being boring and bureaucratic offices, they can become collaborative, efficient spaces centered on the citizens. If no one proposes it, let's make them make it their priority. Because no one is going to be able to solve the problems from this era with that ancient structure they have.

I love to tell this: when I went to Disney World there were still printed tickets to get in. Not anymore. That's outdated. Now you use a bracelet instead of a ticket. And it comes with your name engraved. You can do everything with it. Open your hotel room. Get into the park. Get into exclusive queues. Pay at stores. Get into special areas. This is an enormous example for governments, because there's many more.

It's a whole data analysis science in real time behind the bracelets. Those who are in charge of organizing the park's logistics, have a screen with a map which shows every bracelet location. And here's where the most interesting thing comes in. If they start seeing in the map that one of the park's area begins to crowd or congest, the quickly look for some of the most famous characters, like Mickey or some princess, and they send them to the park's part with less people so they begin to distribute better. That's focusing on the clients having a good experience!

The success from Luis Miguel series was something immense. And it's another story of how a company works for the people of this century.

My friends. My family. People I follow on Twitter. Everyone. Everyone on a Sunday waiting for the next episode. Sales and download from his music skyrocketed by people from all generations. It was his perfect return. In a big way.

Several weeks later after the first season ended, "La Casa de las Flores" starred. And everyone kept doing the challenge of speaking like Paulina de la Mora.

The series being produced for Mexico are no coincidence. Nothing is at Netflix. They have their secrets. And they take risks. What can they lose? Not long ago I read an article published on Harvard Business Review magazine by Michael Smith and Rahul Telang in which they talked about how data analysis can also improve creative projects.

That's how things are. Netflix can know which movies or series you've seen. In which minute you paused them. Or in which part you stopped watching. How many episodes you saw in one day (or how many seasons you saw in one day). So they begin to connect that data. They start making profiles with what you like, your habits and interests. And they focus in presenting you the contact you like. But they're also creating content for you. Enrique Dans, in a Forbes publication, explains how Netflix closes its contracts. For example, when they closed a deal with the Obamas or with Shonda Rhimes to produce series. The amount of those contracts wasn't based on inspiration, a sixth sense, or intuition. It's based on models that show them the probability of success depending on the mix of talent, plot, actors, and other factors. And they not only know the probability of success. They also have a very clear idea of how many of its subscribers are going to watch the new content.

So, nothing of what Netflix is doing is by divine inspiration. If the created a new series or movie is because their data predicted it would work.

We didn't realize it, but when Netflix came to Mexico, it started with a lot of Mexican content. From Televisa, and other producers as well. That's how they do it in every country. They include regional content. But it's not to please us. It's to measure us. Explore the number of people with this or that interest. They make all their measurements with the regional content that already exists. And when they have enough data, they turn on the series and movies factory. They take out the content with which why were testing the audience. And their own creation successes start.

These two examples from Disney and Netflix using technology to its favor are to open our eyes to how far behind the government is. And to realize the lack of leadership that they're on the disposition to make things start to happen in a fast and efficient way. With the youth in their side to achieve all this transformation that's needed within the institutions.

I don't say the government should use the data and technology to keep an eye on us or produce content we like. But I'm talking about using technology to improve cities. Make things easier. Improve communication. Be way more transparent. And make better decisions. I love this topic. As a digital consultant I can think of thousands of solutions that politicians and governors can have. Not just apps. Everything can be done.

There you have the traffic cameras issue. Without getting into discussions or taking postures for or against, the facts were that there were deaths for car accidents in my city due to high speed. It was decided to set radar cameras and form one day to the other they were active and sending tickets to those who went over the speed limit. The program saved close to fifteen lives a year. But they kept to be a public opinion failure. And in any conversation. The team never knew how to communicate the program well.

The complaints everywhere were that the goal was to get more money. And that the ticket was too expensive for people who earned the minimum wage. I never understood that. It's supposed that no one should break the law nor the basic rules. And if someone didn't want to pay tickets, the only thing there was to do was to not go over the speed limit. Way too simple.

They're not active anymore. Like it always happens in Mexico: they act with political reasons. They uninstalled the radars and the program was eliminated. Instead of progressing with more control systems to prevent corruption and solve social problems, like in this case with car accidents, we went backwards.

With situations like these I think about how we will achieve the great changes that the country needs, if in a city with one million inhabitants we couldn't come to an agreement to launch a program from this kind. The majority opposed. Even when it was about saving people's lives. How many good improvement opportunities are we losing due to the lack of dialogue?

The fact that I worked and studied at the same time made me grow a lot more. I had to organize my times. Face reality. Know how the older people are and realize the big difference on how we perceive things and the way we can propose different solutions to the same problems. There's a really big generational gap.

I see it this way. Us millennials are here to find balances.

Work in team. Collaborate. Only we can join our new modern ideas with the experience older people have. If that was accomplished in the workplaces, generations working in team, truly, the results would be very big and much more enriched than if people from just one age would have done it. Like everywhere, the results are also better at work when there's diversity.

I regret something. Not having said many things I thought in all the meetings I was in. Being the youngest one in the team gave me another perspective on many of the topics that were discussed. But regret that the comments I made with good intentions weren't always well received by everyone.

When my friends started to do their internships and we got together and talked about how each of us was doing, we always had a conversation about the meetings. And everyone had something to say about it. That's what happened to me. And what happened to them too.

At first I didn't say anything. It was my first job and I was learning how everything was. On one hand, you want to make a good impression, you don't want to have problems with anyone, and be at peace with everyone. But you also want to give good ideas, say what you agree with and what you don't agree with, and give an opinion on whether you think something is going to work or not.

In my room, there's no WiFi coverage on my phone nor my computer. But oddly there's coverage for my Kindle to connect. I can't comfortably watch Netflix on my bed, but I can look for new books on Amazon. One weekend I found one named "The 5 second rule". It's about how whenever we want to do something, our brain starts to think about reasons not do it. It's our way of protecting ourselves. What they recommend in this book is that next time you want to do something, like say what you think, get up from bed, or finish a task, make a countdown in your head. Like if you were going to launch a rocket. Five. Four. Three. Two. One. Do it! This simple countdown distracts your brain from thinking on the possible dangers, the fears or the possible obstacles.

I did just that in the next meeting after I read that book. When I had something to say, instead of thinking everything that could go wrong or everything they would think about me, I did the countdown inside my head. And I said it. It was a good way so start. It's a little frightening to speak for the first time. There's the nervousness and some worries about what they would say. Remember the five-second rule. If you're afraid, act as if you weren't. No one is going to notice the difference.

I gained confidence with that. And a little after I started to talk and propose. Because of my age or anything else, whatever I said was always "more complicated to do", or very "first world". There was always the one who said the famous phrase: "No, because things have always been done this way". What a big dilemma. Many times I had to internally decide if it was worth speaking, even if no one liked what I said. Or remain silent. Even if I didn't agree.

I wasn't used to any of that. In the meetings I had in different activities and projects from my university it was always encouraged for everyone to give their opinion so things would go the best way.

There were days were the only thing I wanted was to resign. It seemed very complicated trying to convince other people with your ideas about how to improve things. Many of the people who were seated at the meetings were very close-minded. It's very easy to detect when someone likes to be given feedback. And it's even easier to realize when someone gets angry when they comment on their work. That's not my style. It has never been. Nor is it our generation's style. The majority of us like receiving feedback and comments about what we do. To improve it.

Not being listened gets you angry. And it gets you even angrier that because of people who don't listen, things don't go forward as they should. Many nights, when I went to bed and turned everything off, I staying going over the conversations or discussions and I thought about how could I have replied something they said. I knew that everyone else who went to the meetings said everything they thought and left without any worries. And there I was, hours or days after, stressed about what I didn't say. I learned the lesson not to remain silent almost in the end. Because it doesn't matter to have good intentions if there are no good actions. Or that your thinking about everything you could have said at night. But you didn't say it.

Little by little I realized something else: if you're there, it's because you belong there. It's your job to say things and make them work the best possible. If you don't take your role and your own opinions seriously, no one else will. So in the next meeting or the next time you have a project or an important opinion, raise your voice and say what you have to say the loudest you can.

It's always going to be a good strategy to talk and say

everything you think. That's your added value. Your experience and everything you've been through are going to define your ideas. And they are needed! That's why someone trusted you to be there. Staying quiet is already failing. If you're in a team, it's your job to make things go as good as possible. And as a citizen, it also has to be.

I keep the memory of being the youngest one in the team and the most stubborn in thinking that things could be done in a different way. Every time they saw me arriving they called me *minion* for being millennial. In our last months of work, the Mayor asked me about what I thought was best on certain topics. The first time he did it I almost drop my phone. And I texted his wife telling her how excited I was because he had asked for my opinion in front of everyone.

If in your school, at work, in your organization or in your own company you don't like the activities there are, create one. That's what I did when I didn't like the other student groups. Or look for what can be improved, like I did in my job. But always, always, participate giving an extra from you. Without staying quiet. Mexico, your company, your institution or any other organization you're part of need your revolutionary ideas. And your way of doing things. Because the ones from other haven't worked.

Every time you do that you're going to find people who will oppose. Take my experience on that. And reality is that those people who stop change, are in private companies as much as in public institutions. In Mexico and any country. But I do think it's our job to make things happen. Being empathetic can help you think about reasons why someone opposes something. And never take it personal.

Defend the person you are. Express your ideas. Feel proud about your way of doing things. Keep an open mind. Talk. Say everything you have to say. And listen. Invest time in you. Look what else can you get involved with. Think about what else can be done, beside what's already done.

Now every time someone calls me millennial, trying to make some kind of mockery, I take it to my favor.

Yes. I'm millennial.

I'm hurried trying to find solutions that help us all. The problems are many, they're big and serious to be losing time.

We have to act fast. We're not going to be sitting in an

office all day long when we can be looking for ideas, working in teams, eliminating barriers that stop us from the change we so want and need.

And making things happen.

PART OF A
WORLD

"If it scares you, it might be a good thing to try."

-

Seth Godin

The Magic of The Mermaid

Just the day I arrived to Warsaw, in Poland, I saw that the city was full of blue flags with a compass in the middle with the four cardinal points. It was the North Atlantic Treaty Organization's logo. A military organization that was created during the cold war. It seemed weird that every post had one. But I was so tired because of the trip I had done to get there, that the only thing I did was arrive at the hotel, take a shower, and set up my things. It was a Sunday. And there were a few hours left to rest before summer classes started the next day. Showering with hot water is always a good idea to regain energy.

I couldn't believe it. I was finally in Europe. For real, I've had wanted to go for years. And the idea of studying there was never in my plans.

Applying to that summer program, one day before enrollment was closed, was one of the best things I've done. Those things that happen without thinking or planning. And I wasn't alone. I had my mom's support, my grandparents' and my aunts' and uncles'. Before I left, they called me to invite me to have lunch or dinner at their house. When I got there they gave me an envelope with dollars or euros so I could cover expenses (the early birthday and Christmas gifts). I also didn't feel alone when I asked for the special permit at my job. Very nervous, one night, I went to the Mayor and his wife's home. I told them I had to talk really seriously with them. I talked to them about the idea I had of going to study abroad for almost two months. And to my surprise they got more excited than me. They told me not to worry and to apply. I could do many things from my computer, no matter where I was.

So there I was. Fulfilling one more dream.

During the rest of the day, the rest of the students who were in the program started to arrive. We were all Mexicans. And from the Tec. But from different cities and campuses. We had only met through the messages we had sent over a WhatsApp group. We were introducing ourselves and then we went out to get to know the city. After eating, the second most important thing: get internet. No one had. After looking for several options, we found some phone sim cards which costed ten zlotys, that's like fifty pesos. And they gave us 12 gigabytes to use. The cheapest internet of my life. We went back to the hotel and we all went to our rooms. The university coordinators send us the instructions and the next day schedule through Facebook. I almost couldn't sleep due to the excitement.

The sun went down at eleven at night. And it came out from three or four in the morning. We came down at eight. I loved breakfast. There was a lot of variety to make many different combinations every day and not repeat. And it was healthy. There were veggies, egg, fruits and many different kinds of sausages. Even some black ones no one wanted to try. At the tables we were still talking about us and where were we from.

Lukaz arrived after breakfast, he was the coordinator of the program. He was like thirty years old. On the first tour he gave us around the university and the important places of the city, we realized he was passionate about history. And we all liked him.

There was also Kassia (a Marilyn Monroe replica). She

was still a student, but taking care of us was part of her social service or something like that. She is one of the most kind and sincere people I know. And Annia, also a student. More responsible but more direct and straightforward. We could ask them anything. And they liked to go out and talk to us.

After taking several busses and walking a little, we got to school. The University of Warsaw. I simply loved it. The entrance is as elegant and inspiring as the ones from the best universities. It has an eagle with a crown, surrounded by five starts. And there are statues of Athena and Urania to the sides. It's supposed that when you enter, you're under the protection of the wisdom Goddess and the university knowledge Goddess. They built it in 1816. So you could imagine the kind and style of architecture it has.

We finished the tour and Lukaz invited us to a restaurant in the city center. Without asking he asked for vodka shots for everyone. He wanted to make sure we tried the best one. Then we kept walking and tasting the street food while he told us some interesting facts about the city. The city center was beautiful, the most colorful and picturesque I remember.

As I was walking I saw that every lamp post had the

NATO flags. So I asked Kassia about it. As if I needed even more things to make my excitement bigger about being there, she told me there would be a convention with all the Heads of State who are part of NATO. That's why the whole city was getting prepared for that.

Until then, it had been the best trip of my life.

Several days before, I had been in London. I got there just in the morning they were waking up with the news about Brexit becoming official. The voting across the whole United Kingdom had happened the night before. The King Cross train station was the first thing I visited because I arrived there. But from there I went straight to 10 Downing Street. The building where the Prime Minister lives while he's in charge (the kind of places that, according to my friends, only I like). David Cameron was the Prime Minister then. I couldn't get very close due to the amount of journalists who where there waiting for some official statement. A few hours later I knew, because of the news, that just at that place where I had been waiting, he came out to announce his resignation. David had asked for the support and vote from the English people to stay in the European Union. But the option to exit had won, with 52% of the votes. To him, it meant a leadership loss.

Of course I also visited Tower Bridge, the Buckingham Palace and Soho. I even saw the Wicked musical and took pictures in front of the theatre were Harry Potter's play is showing.

After London, I was in Brussels, or as they call it, Europe's capital, because practically there's where politics and actions from the European Union are decided. The Parlamentarium museum is perfect for anyone like me who wants to know more details and getting in depth on the EU topic. It's interactive and modern. There was a giant gallery on the roof outside with photos from world leaders like Malala. Another place to get inspired.

In the middle of the Grand Place I felt I had traveled back in time to the fifteenth century. It was almost ten minutes away walking. So wherever I was going, I had to go through there. On the contrary, when I was under the giant metal molecule called Atomium, I felt I was in 2050.

And I don't forget I spent an entire day trying to get to the NATO headquarters. It has a giant esplanade with the countries that are members. But due to some transport system repairs I wasn't able to get there. I was desperate, but nothing that the best waffles in the world or some french fries couldn't calm. There I didn't know that, even though I wasn't able to visit NATO, NATO would go to me.

NATO was born in 1949 as a group of allied European countries. And one more: United States. The organization's goal back then was to create a big group of countries to promote the democratic system against the communist one. They were also military allies. If something happened, they would defend each other like one. In response to NATO, the soviet countries signed in 1955 the Warsaw Pact and the Soviet Union was created. Even though it would have seemed totally impossible for it to happen before, after all they suffered and achieved to become a democracy, Poland joined NATO in 1997.

Things are now way different that to the Cold War time. Now even Trump threatens his allies to get them out of this organization if they don't pay what they owe for the military protection they have given them. So don't worry. We're not the only country with conflicts with their neighbors.

Now in Poland, on top of the things I had already planned, I had the opportunity of "casually" meeting with one or several of the world's most important leaders. Barack Obama, Justin Trudeau, Angela Merkel, and other

25 chiefs of state and government, gathered, to discuss topics about security, military presence, migration crisis, nuclear disarmament and others. All of them at a convention in the city where I was going to spend the rest of the summer. I had to do something to meet them. And, if it was not enough, even Pope Francis was going to visit Poland that same month to celebrate the World Youth Day.

Officially, that trip had become the best of my whole life. How well had Europe received me!

In one of the buses we took daily to go to the university, we saw something we didn't expect. A Polish senior lady, with a red hat with the PRI logo. It was a hat from Zedillo's presidential campaign! How did it get all the way there? And why was she using it? It was something really weird. And we never knew how it happened because the lady didn't speak English. So we could only laugh for a while and keep on our way to class.

I had the most inspiring teachers at the University of Warsaw. We studied topics like multiculturalism, migration, and international law. And the topic that was never missing in a class (or news program): Brexit. The world wanted to know what was going to happen. After all the European union is the only supranational organism in the world and back them it was going through a crisis in which everyone questioned if its purposed could be achieved or not.

Winston Churchill's dream was a United Europe. Or how he called it, the United European States.

The European Union's motto is "United in diversity". One only anthem. One only currency. One only flag. One only economy. One only commercial partner for the rest of the world. One only passport. And the free flow of its inhabitants. Nowadays every country with their own internal problems. There was the economic recession in Greece. Great Britain had just voted to exit. Italy wasn't growing while Portugal did it to half of what it was expected. And summing all of that, there was, and still is, they great migration problem.

Jan Zielonka, professor at Oxford University, published an article about everything that the European Union was expected to be when it started. Like being the most competitive economy in the world. The "consensus of Stockholm" was also supposed to prevail above the "consensus of Washington". The good results they have obtained aren't put aside, but it reduces to a few countries and a few topics. Like the good economic performance that Germany, Austria, and the Netherlands have had. The euro, as he explains, seemed like a success at the beginning. One only currency achieved to protect Europe from financial volatility. But now it seems that using the same currency achieved then contrary. It made noticeable the differences and the conflicts between countries with a surplus and deficit, the importers and exporters, the North and the South. And his article ends by saying how one of the purposes was also to end with political power. And now we see how Europe's politics is still led by the powerful and rich countries.

In Brussels, the tour guide from the tour I took, gave us her opinion about that. From her perspective, the European Union should have started by a cultural union. And that's how what's happening could have been prevented.

It's still impossible to know if it will work. But no one can say they're not trying. If they achieve it, who says that Mexico can't be the leader of a Latin American union in the future.

Mexico has many similarities with Poland. Most part of the population belongs to the catholic religion. And it's one of the few countries in the European Union with an economy that's mainly dedicated to the manufacturing industry. Even the prices are basically the same (but in zlotys). It was a relief for my wallet when I got there and stopped spending 10 pounds for a hamburger and fries meal.

On the streets, the cars I saw passing by weren't all luxury nor from really exclusive brands. Like in London where many Mercedes Benz cars or Range Rovers pass by every second. And the streets aren't fashion runways like in Paris. But people are from another world.

After I step foot in that country I could notice something. Even though the new generations, the youngest ones, are inspiringly passionate, energized, and globalized, the oldest ones, the senior people, are the contrary.

You could make friends everywhere. People my age were open to hear your story and everything you had to tell. Always smiling. And they love Mexicans (wherever). Even though I had just met them, they got excited and told me what they did and what their goals were. And we exchanged our contacts to hang out later. They got me full of energy and good vibes. Hopefully in Mexico we get to a point like that, in which we all feel excited and passionate about what each of us does.

And there's the senior people. It wasn't like that with them. They're absolutely different.

The first say I got there, because I didn't have internet, I couldn't find out how to get to the hotel. I imagine that because it was early, there were not so many people from my age awake. But there was a lot of senior people. After a while I learned why, but that first day I only saw serious and severe faces. Very strong looks. Like if they were very angry all the time or planning to do something bad. I got a bit afraid. And when I finally got the courage to talk to someone to ask which bus I had to take, they only shared their head to tell me no. They didn't understand English. And their face told me that me talking to them had bothered them.

Even though I found similarities between Mexico and Poland, our stories are totally different. I went from fear to compassion when I understood, being there, how recent the end of the Cold War was, the fall of Berlin's Wall, and communism absolution. And before that, the holocaust. Maybe it's because studying about that era in books or seeing it only in movies or documentaries, we think it was centuries ago. And maybe us Mexicans see it even more distant because we didn't suffer any of that.

We're fortunate. Our independence was in 1810. Poland even disappeared from the map on one occasion, and it was until 1918, a hundred years after, when thanks to some events like the Russian Revolution, Germany's defeat and the end of the Austro-Hungarian Empire, that they could claim their independence. They suffered the Nazi invasion almost immediately. And the horrors from WWII after that. They endured one thing after the other.

Senior people reflect that. They say everything with their eyes and gazes. Their hearts are still filled with all the suffering and the horrors they and their families lived. They're not used to foreigners. They don't like them. And that's perfectly understandable. They were attacking them over and over again.

And if something could open my eyes even more to understand that, was the visit to the Auschwitz concentration camps. Some people of the group didn't even know if we were going to be able to get in. We were all very quiet. The day of our visit was cloudy. Very dark. On the way there I felt I lost energy every time we were getting closer. And just when we got to the place, it started raining. We got off the bus we took there, and without saying anything, we walked to the entrance. I recognized the place immediately. I had seen it before in many movies and documentaries. Now it was real. I was present there. I felt sadness and frustration. It wasn't just a concentration camp. It was an extermination camp. A place that will always be a symbol of terror and genocide. One of the worst places in the history of humanity.

There was the rounded sign which said "Arbeit macht frei". Work will make you free. The cruel and iconic phrase at the entrance of that and many other nazi concentration camps. And I started the same route that many jews and Polish people had been forced to take. Walking by that place was walking where a few more than a million people were exterminated. I was watching with my own eyes what they all had seen for the last time in their lives.

I wish I could erase from my mind that I entered the same basements and the same gas cameras where many families had been taken for being murdered later. I can't imagine what they felt when they were there. In their last seconds of life. Waiting for what they feared the most to happen. With the last memories and images from their parents, their kids or their siblings on their mind. Thinking about everything that could have been. But wasn't. And what was about to end the worst way possible.

We have to learn from history. Even from the horrific moments in it. There's always going to be the possibility of it repeating itself. "If it already happened, it can happen again", is written in one of the walls.

Because of what happened there, there are many incomplete families today. That's why everything is still present in their hearts. Because they are the survivors from that terrible era. Seniors from that country, and from some others, are the parents who lost their kids. Or are the sons or daughters who lost their parents. Even though we find them cold and distant, what they would like the most is to go back in history to be with their loved ones again who were taken away from them in a horrible way. They wished to be in peace with them. Happy. Hugging them.

Although maybe because of their semblance we saw that they didn't like us being in their country, we had a profound respect for them. There have been enormously strong and resilient. And they have managed to improve the situation they saw so that future generations are better than they were. And they haven't had to wait years to see those changes. They already saw how it is to live in a democracy. With a vibrant and energized youth. In a united Europe.

And in a time in which, finally, they don't have to hide or live with fear. Maybe deep down those faces, and serious gazes, there are smiles. Maybe they tell themselves: "We got over it. We did well. We made it".

Some days after my visit to Auschwitz, the world saw in the news Pope Francis' historic visit to that same concentration camp. Never before had another one visited that place. He did a silent tour. A reflection tour. And of prayer. I understand it. There's not much to say when you're there. And, on the contrary, there's much to think about. "I'd like to go to that place of horror without speeches, without crowds. Alone. Get in. Pray. And let the Lord give me the grace to cry", he said before arriving. After doing it, his only public words were the ones he wrote on the visitors' book: "Lord, have mercy of your people. Lord, forgive such cruelty".

I had never seen it this way: 51% of the population in the whole world is less than 30 years old. We the youth are majority! We could change things if we want to. Seriously.

But there's a problem here. From the thousands of congressmen, representatives and people in public office, only 2% are that age or are from this generation. We can't do much if it stays like this.

In 2016 the United Nations launched a campaign called "Not Too Young to Run" to get many more young people to participate in their country's important decisions. And they are trying to do it the best way: motivating them to run for public office. The catchy phrase from the campaign was: "We think that, if you're young enough to vote, you're young enough to run for office". That same year I met two people in Poland who gave an impulse to that UN cause. And they made me believe, even more, that us young people shouldn't set ourselves limits. Nor stop acting.

One of Warsaw's most emblematic buildings is the Palace of Culture and Science. It was built in 1955. With the first look you take, you realize that it has an absolute soviet design. With that country's history, it has been hard not to demolish it. Because it's a bad memory from the communist era. If they haven't done it, is not to forget their past. And avoid it from happening again. Now it's the place for different kind of offices, bookstores, movie theaters, and it even has a pool. I put on my favorite clothes to go there: a white shirt, blue pants and brown shoes. Simple. We went up in that impressive building's elevator. And just in the floor where you can see the entire city through the windows we met a girl more or less my age. Blond hair. Black blazer. I thought she was the assistant of the person we were looking for. Until Lukaz, who came along with us, formally introduced her to us. It was her! Aleksandra Gajewska. At 21 she won her first election to become deputy for the city council. What in Mexico would be a councillor. I instantaneously felt a great admiration for her.

We sat in a very executive room. Where she and the other deputies have their meetings. But now it was all for us. Each desk had a microphone so everyone could hear your voice. Aleksandra told us how she won, the job she took care of and how government and politics worked in Poland. Like in classes, I was the only one taking notes about everything and asking questions. I was very excited for everything that I was learning. But even more because I had someone in front of me who was the living demonstration, that if, you're old enough to vote, you're old enough to be voted, like the UN campaign said.

She's still one of my best examples to follow. For what Lukaz told us, Aleksandra has won the respect of many politicians and governors from Poland. And now I realized why. She seemed my age, but she also seemed the most professional, diplomatic, and local public politics expert person. And she was. IN the end I took a photo with her and I posted it on my Instagram account with the hashtag #HillaryClinton2 along with my prediction that she will be Poland's next President. I still bet she will.

That night I couldn't sleep.

I took a black journal from my briefcase that I had bought at a market in Edinburgh. I grabbed my computer. And I went down to the hotel bar. Not to drink vodka. To work with a nice coffee. I had so many ideas. If I didn't take the opportunity to write them down, I would forget and never do them. In one sheet of paper I write down what I was coming up with to do at my job when I went back to Mexico. In another sheet, I wrote "book topics". It was the first brainstorming for a future book about everything that the young people of the country think and what can we do to change it. Even though I started writing it just two years later, that's where everything that you're now reading started. I haven't lost hope on our generation since then.

Later that night we met at a room. We ordered pizza. We went to buy chips (with no flavor) and a jalapeño-flavored Tabasco sauce bottle (the only one we found).

They tasted awful. But it was the closest thing we found to something spicy and sour. And we spent all night talking and laughing like crazy, drinking coca cola in coffee mugs and trying to open a wine bottle with a shoe. With no success.

Those were good times.

And the inspiring people didn't stop showing up. In one of those days of classes at the University of Warsaw, King Gajewska also came to the classroom to tell us her story. But we didn't last long in there. She took us out of the classroom and we went walking to the place where she worked.

She went for the big one. She didn't see limits, she believes in herself and her capacity to represent a whole country. And at 24 years old she launched her campaign to become a member of the parliament. Not Poland's. She believed so much in her power for making a change, that she ran to be in the European Parliament. She told us that she was studying back then. She expected her classmates and professors to support her. But it wasn't like that. IN the middle of her campaign, they mocked her. They told her she was obviously going to lose. A professor talked to her very seriously and bet she wouldn't get even a thousand votes. Twenty-first century and adults trying to discourage the youngest ones? No, thank you.

In fact, she lost the election. But her story didn't end there. When she lost, she won the respect of those who made fun of her. Because even though she didn't get to the European Parliament, she got much more votes than they thought she would. They said they were sorry. They congratulated her. And they cheered her up so she would try it again.

A few blocks after, we arrived to the Parliament by foot. Because the nest year after she lost, she ran again and won the election to be a member of Poland's Parliament. In Mexico it would be like the Republic's Senate. 25 years old and already in the Senate! I follow her on Instagram. On the photos she posts, with other national and international leaders, she's always the youngest one. And the most promising.

If she would have been worried about what her classmates and acquaintances would think, she would have probably never ran for anything. If she wasn't strong enough to accept the first results, see what she had done wrong, and take energy to do it again, she would have never arrived to the office she has now with which she can represent a great part of the population and make decisions that affect the entire country. And what excites me the most is that she's there to represent the young people from my generation and women.

I noticed something special about her; she was very authentic. Transparent. Not shy. That's what young people in Mexico have to do. Love what we do. And be ourselves. Sometimes you try to act like someone older or someone different to fit into some stereotype. Like some job position. She had the option to behave like the other politicians that were with her in the senate. All of them older than fifty or sixty. Serious. Boring. And reserved. But if something has made her win the trust of her voters, is that she's herself. It's reflected on every speech she gives, in every cause she supports and in every initiative she votes.

There are many lessons to learn on how to be strong and resilient in her story. Mostly, if you're one of the few young people in Mexico who has just ran for public office, without success (Pedro Kumamoto). You have to know this: your story changing Mexico isn't over. Just like her story didn't end on her first defeat. And if you're one of those who have never participated in an election, but you see a possibility, even if small, of running one day for public office, because you trust your capacity to improve things, you have to know there will be a lot of people who won't support you and will do everything to discourage you, and a lot of people will bet everything on you and the change you represent. But who's stronger? In the end, always, the one who does good. Maybe it works on the first try. Maybe until the second one, third or fourth. Adam Grant, one of my favorite writers, tweeted something about that:

> *"If you define success in terms of winning or losing, you already lost".*

If you define them in terms of learning, you've already won. Because you can do an analysis of what happened in every failure. And with that you would have learned the great lesson life wanted to give you. And you will know how to do it better on the next try.

It depends on you. Any plan you have. And no matter how hard or unattainable it seems, dare to do it.

Mexico and the countries from all around the world needs young people to start fulfilling their dreams.

I looked the schedules and hotels in which the heads of

State were staying. There wasn't a lot of information. The NATO conventions are private. There were security deployments everywhere those days. Three or four helicopters on the sky. Closed streets. Route changes in public transport. That bothered Polish people. They believed that when all the Presidents and Prime Ministers were gathered, there would be a Russian terrorist attack. A bomb or something. I was more excited every time about the unique change to meet them.

Kassia had told us that during that week she wouldn't be able to come with us. She was going to be working as an intern at the NATO summit. I begged her to tell me more details. Even though she's the kindest and smiling person I've met in my life, she couldn't tell us anything. She had signed a non-disclosure agreement. Her professionalism, before anything else. She couldn't even tell us what her job was there.

Online, I found the time Obama was going to land. Mi hotel was just on the highway to the airport. It was a good spot to try to see everything that happened. It was 2am and I went down to the lobby. There was a crowd. And all the national channels were installed just there. While Obama arrived, I started talking to the ones outside. Something really easy to do with Polish people.

Screams started to be heard. And everyone started moving. Something like fifty motorcycles passed by and then fifty cars from Warsaw's police. All of them with their titling blue and red lights. Then, like twenty black Suburbans. Two helicopters. And then "The Beast" passed by. That's what they call the United States President's car. The safest in the world. It can survive crashes, attacks, and they even say it has weapons included. Like in James Bond's movies. I recorded everything. The car didn't stop. It was night and you couldn't see through the window. But I would have more days to chase him. And get a selfie.

When I woke up, I saw an Instagram photo with Obama going to have breakfast at a Mexican restaurant in Warsaw City Center. How was I not there? I decided it wasn't going to happen again, so I stayed for hours waiting for him to arrive at his hotel's entrance. But his security team had another entrance to keep him safe. It seemed impossible to approach him. I left. After I gave up, another friend from the Mexican group did the same. He was waiting for several hours at the same place until he also realized it was impossible.

During the days the convention lasted, the presidents

and heads of state discussed topics on nuclear arms, migration, military troop positions, and more topics that had to do with European countries' security. In the end, we couldn't see any of them.

Bad luck.

But no one took away from us the excitement of being in the most important city in the world at that moment. They mentioned it in every news program. At least on Twitter we could see all them giving statements and speeches. The background full of flags.

Poland is a whole example. With its devastating history, they are progressing. Their growth may not be the same as China's, Korea's or that from other European regions. But they also haven't had the same history as them. We have to be fair with comparisons. And yes. They are growing much more than Mexico. Yet with the fact that history has been kinder to us.

We were a country that was progressing in the nineties. In fact, we have done it in every era. 1810: our independence started and the path to our liberty. A hundred years later: the revolution. And we have lived in a democracy ever since (there are some signals that make it seem like we're about to lose it; we can't let that happen).

Countries with less than twenty or thirty years with that government system are already getting ahead of us.

When did we get stuck?

We don't have to hit rock bottom to react. And I don't like to hear people who even feel proud saying things are going to stay the same. Those who say it's not worth trying. Or participating in NGOs. Or demanding the government or participating in it. Or doing things right. Those who are corrupt because they think everyone else is.

And every time I think that young people can't do anything to change this, I remember Kinga and Alexandra's stories. Two women. The bravest from their generation. Achieving more every time.

Every time I think Mexico will never be able to move forward, I remember the little time in which Poland has recovered from its devastating history. And every time I think I'm doing something insignificant, I remember how over there anyone, whatever they did, was totally committed and proud of it.

That's why I didn't want to leave. It was a place that changed me. It made me see things differently and believe more that anyone, despite their age, can change the world.

But I had to go back to work.

To finish the semesters, I had left to get my degree. And keep on with my life.

Much more inspired than ever.

"If you do what you've always done, you'll get what you've always gotten."

–

Tony Robbins

Crossing The Han River

What a coincidence! It was June 21. I had taken my flight to Europe that day one year ago.

And now, just that same day, I was taking a flight to Asia. What could I do? I loved to travel.

After visiting Tokyo for several days, I got to the University of Seoul, in Korea. They gave us the keys, and each one went looking for their room. When I got in, the first thing I realized was that the beds had no pillows nor sheets. After arriving from a long trip, the first thing you want to do is leave all your things. Rest a little. Relax. And get out know the city. It seemed like a joke. Everyone was already in a bad moon in the hallways.

Like in other programs, the university assigned us Korean students to help us get installed and adapted to the culture. So because this time we were more than 150 foreign students, there were much more Koreans with us. We called them *seoulmates* (because of the city's name).

They were with a face full of doubt when we came down to the dorms lobby and asked them about our beds. Apparently, they had sent us an e-mail several weeks before, telling us we had to bring our own sheets, pillows, and blankets with us. Even though the mail had gotten lost (like some homework which never makes it to the professor), I wasn't going to come all the way from Mexico carrying sheets. I always travel light. Just with a carry-on that fits the overhead compartment in the plane.

At night, my *seoulmate* and I, went walking to one of the closes shopping malls. We were talking about our countries and their differences. He told me he liked tacos, and that he had taken Spanish classes. I got a little bit embarrassed because it seemed that my *seoulmate* knew a lot more about Mexican culture than I knew about Korean culture.

We got to Lotte Mart, which would be something like Walmart or Target. Back then I didn't know I would keep seeing that brand everywhere. Lotte has buildings, sweets, hamburgers, movie theaters and shopping malls. Even an amusement park called Lotte World, with a castle in the middle. Has someone seen the similarity with Disney World? I left realizing that the companies over there are really diversified. Like Samsung. We know their phones and some of the home appliances they make. But in Korea they sell their own cars.

Even though we had gone in separate groups, all the foreigners from the summer program were there at Lotte Mart. Buying the same thing. Some with the whole package of sheets, blankets, and pillows. Some others didn't want to spend a lot and they got the smallest and hardest pillow they found and a blanket. At the towel department we didn't know if we should laugh or cry. The only ones they had, were the size we use in Mexico to dry our hands in the bathroom. Oh well. There was no choice. We payed and looked for the first food spot open at that time. And then we got back exhausted to the university. Straight to our dorms. Finally, we could lay down.

On the Facebook group we had, the professors asked who wanted to volunteer to give the welcome speech the nest day. I replied with a comment on the post that I was up for it. I had some ideas. But I was so tired that I slept. I wrote the speech when I woke up. And practiced it. I wanted to say something everyone could relate to, no matter which country they came from.

They introduced me and the first thing I said when I stood behind the podium was this: "I hope at this moment everyone already has their sheets and pillows after the panic shopping last midnight". First, that had stressed us all out and put us in a bad mood. Now it had become our inside joke. I also wanted to thank the *seoulmates*. They put a lot of effort on helping us and being available anytime. And I was very excited because of the classes I was going to take and the places I was going to visit. In Mexico, I had already studied Korea's success case. 50 years ago, they were among the poorest countries in the world. In fact, their economy compared to some of the countries in Africa. Now it's one of the best and strongest. It's one of the stories I like to tell the most. Besides, I want the success Korea had, for Mexico.

"Seoul is an impressive city. And Korea is a country with an outstanding history. With a unique present. And a very promising future. I'm from Mexico. But it really doesn't matter where we come from. We all have a lot to learn from Korea", I also said.

As I talked, I realized the great opportunity I was living. Getting there wasn't easy at all for me. When I got accepted by the University of Seoul, I applied for a government scholarship I thought I was going to win but didn't. I had to adjust all my spending. And this time, in my job, I took longer to get the Mayor to give me permission for not going during the whole summer. Because of that in the speech I also talked about how important it is to get out of your comfort zone. And about how all the success stories around the world confirm that when you get out of it, incredible things start happening in your life.

I was ready to learn the Korean way of doing things. But I didn't even know where to start. I enrolled in History and Politics of Korea, Doing Business in Asia and Urbanization classes. It seemed to me those were the perfect subjects to take notes, keep asking questions, getting into detail, and apply what I had learned in Mexico.

But not everything was about the classes.

Along with Karen, who I had just met, I did a list of all the places where we had to go. We basically put them all. In a shared Google Drive file we ordered the places by location. We had to use a printed map, old school, because Google Maps didn't work in Korea. We put a day and hour to every place. We were both decided not to miss any touristic or historic place. So the schedule was already full.

Seoul is the world's biggest city. But to our good luck, it's also the city with the best public transportation system. Punctual, and with the capacity to connect every point of the city in a perfect and efficient way. We only had to walk a few blocks to get to the closest metro station from the university. Make some connections. And get wherever we wanted to.

I don't even know how to say it. I love Korea. And there's really a big stereotype. Many of the people I know, when I told them I was going to go, they imagined I was going to eat gross and slimy food on the street. That I was going to have to deal with non-civilized people. With dirty places. And that I was going to have to make signs and shout to get myself understood.

None of that. I felt in one of the most modern places I have visited in my life.

The first view I had from Korea was when I was about to land at the Incheon Airport. The fatigue from the trip didn't stop me from me getting excited when I saw the giant, modern, and impressive construction through the window. It's silver. With circular and rounded shapes. From 2005 it has been recognized every year as the best airport in the world. "If this is how the airport is, I can't imagine how the city will be", I thought. And it was true. I got my luggage, I processed my entry to the country at a screen, and I took a train to Seoul. The landscapes I was seeing where beautiful. After thirty minutes, I started to see the streets. All clean, like brand new. And with all the lines and pedestrian signs like they were just painted. We started to stop at different stations. Every time the doors opened, I saw how all the stations also seemed brand new. And very modern.

As I got to the station where I had to get off, I talked to some people. Koreans are extremely educated. Kind and courteous. In the disposition to help. Like when we got lost. We could approach anyone, and on all the times we did, they stopped what they were doing and came with us to where we wanted to go.

And I never felt unsafe. Many of the coffee shops and stores are open twenty-four hours. From a British government report about safety and crime in Korea, it mentions there have been "occasional, isolated, and rare cases of assault". In the conversations I had with Koreans, I always brought up the topic about safety. I wanted to know what they did to get those really low insecurity indexes. But no one could explain it to me. Maybe being in peace is already part of their culture and lifestyle. Instead of having to watch my stuff because someone might steal them or being worried about walking alone at night, I also relaxed. I could be at peace. Like them.

Until I was at the DMZ. There I did felt I was the perfect target to get shot.

It was curious. The war between South Korea and North Korea is not over yet. They signed an amniotic in 1953, to stop the attacks. But they haven't signed peace to this date. Since then, the Demilitarized Zone was born. The most dangerous border in the world, just in the thirty-eight north parallel.

Both countries, according to the agreement, have to maintain their troops to a minimum of two thousand meters from the line that divides them. And there's a small blue colored room just in the middle. The Joint Security Area, that is property of the United Nations. Half the room is occupying North Korean territory, and the other half South Korean territory. Inside, there's a desk for when they meet to do negotiations. And the desk is also with one half in one country, and the other half in the other.

I already knew that place was dangerous. But because I had seen pictures from international diplomats visiting that place, I couldn't simply not go. Only this time, the situation was a little tense.

One month before, North Korea had launched four missiles to attack its enemies' boats. They didn't achieve to do it. And after, they declared those were test launches. But they had drawn the attention and generated tension in the negotiations that were taking place in the UN during those days.

Nervous, I followed the military's orders. It was cloudy, like it had been for the whole month. And there was a little rain that didn't stop us. I was silent during the whole way. In one of the areas, there was music from the sixties playing to the loudest you can imagine. It looked like a horror scene. The shots could be kilometers away and we didn't realize that. But the reason for that music, according to the explanation they gave us, was so that North Korean military doesn't try to hear the conversations the South Korean military has in those headquarters.

With some binoculars we could see what was beyond

the line that divides us.

Even though they occupy similar territories, the differences that parallel sets, are enormous. North Korea is still one of the poorest countries in the world. And they have a socialist and oppressive government.

South Korea has had to take some measures for anything that could happen.

The metro stations, at the entrance, have a symbol that indicates that the station is ready to function as a refuge in case of war or any tragedy. And on the walls, behind the seats from every train car there are glass cabinets that keep gas masks and body protections. And men have to dedicate a year at military school when they reach age majority. All without exception.

But things in Asia change really fast. A professor told us what he was teaching at that moment, even though it was the most recent, surely was already obsolete. They're countries with very dynamic people and economies.

During the time I was writing this book, something unexpected happened. Since his campaign, President Moon Jae-in, talked about his intentions to approach Kim Jong-Un, North Korea's supreme leader, to try to unify the countries in only one. Or at least to try to end once and for all the war that had extended for more than 60 years.

I underestimated the idea of peace and unification. I thought it was practically impossible. Until I saw the two chiefs of state, Moon and Kin, crossing the Demilitarized Zone line and sharing a handshake. Both smiling. To then cross to the other side and do the same thing. It was a big act that all Koreans from one or two generations would have never imagined to be possible! And they already started the talks and agreements to soon sign the so expected peace agreement.

Maybe the Demilitarized Zone will soon no longer exist.

When the evening classes where over, I walked to the dorms. I loved the university. It was full of trees, different building styles, some ancient ones and some very modern, and a lake with a wooden bridge. When I got to my room, I set the alarm and I slept for about forty-five minutes. After, Karen and I met downstairs, at the lobby, to visit whatever was scheduled for that day.

According to my phone, we got to walk up to fifteen or twenty kilometers daily. I do believe that. But the places we visited were worth it. We took a lot of pictures. We went to museums, temples, palaces and exaggeratedly modern new buildings. And we ate a lot. Some times at McDonald's, but most of the time we looked for Korean food. When I was angry it was the first thing I craved. And we tasted so many Korean restaurants that in the end we could choose which one had the most delicious Korean BBQ of all.

There were some places we had to visit at day and night. Like the palaces or temples that looked spectacular with the architectural lighting. That why we got to the dorms at eleven or midnight. My roomie got there almost at the same time as me. Always with bags full of weird and exotic food like octopus lollipops, squid chips or beverages with bean flavor. And we slept even later trying that food he took and talking about the places each one had visited.

There were two types of mornings: on some, I got up one hour before class and I went to Pablo's room, a French friend, in my pajamas. He always prepared espresso coffee and invited me and Martin, from Slovenia, to taste it. But most of the time we couldn't wake up. We both had Urbanization classes early in the morning. We always got to class running because we were always tired and with no sleep. I stopped by the cafeteria to buy a kimbap. it's like sushi, but in one single piece with a triangle shape. And two cans of cold coffee.

The professor had an impressive curriculum. In that moment he was counselor for several government projects. And because the city was perfect for pedestrians and also had the best public transport system in the whole world, there's no better place to learn how it should be done.

I tried to pay attention to his classes all the time.

In Mexico it stills happens to me that I'm walking and when I want to cross a street by the marked lines for pedestrians, it's almost impossible. And when cars stop passing by and I cross to get to the other side, the cars that are coming don't break. It seems like they go faster when they see you crossing. And there's still the belief that pedestrian bridges are a good option. There was not a single one in Korea. People who walk and use a bike or the public transport, have a preference. By far. We have to get to that too. Maybe we can achieve it when those who get to public office are people with the necessary qualifications for the tasks they are supposed to do.

When the class ended, we had one hour to eat. The menu was always different. But it was always Korean food. It was a delight. There's a food called kimchi. It's fermented and condiments cabbage. It serves as a complement for all foods (unlimited). At first I couldn't bear its strong flavor because it tastes like vinegar with pepper. They told us it was one of the healthiest foods. After I googled all of its properties, I couldn't stop eating it. Half way on the summer I already bought my own kimchi jars to have in my backpack.

Because we all had different classes during the day, we all met at the cafeteria to talk for a bit about how it was going. And to make plans for afternoons. I even hurried because from there I went to the "Korean History and Politics" class.

The professor, on the first day, made a question for the whole classroom. "Put up your hand if you think participating in politics is bad". Ok. If they have such and incredible country, it must be because they are informed and they participate. But everyone put their hand up. Everyone, but me, thought participating in politics was bad. "Like many of you", the professor started saying, "one of the first things my dad told me before he died, was that I never got involved in politics. Do you know why?". Some nodded. "To not harm our family's honor", he finished.

In Korea and the majority of Asian countries, the culture is based on Buddhism and Confucianism. They insist a lot that, to have a respectable lifestyle, you have to be diligent, modern, and stoic. That is, maintain your honor and your family's intact. Any lie, mistake, scandal, or failure you have, you stay marked for life. For generations. I had read something about this. But what took me by surprise is that even on the other side of the world, politics is seen as something corrupt and obscure. I didn't understand how they have become one of the world's best countries, if people prefer not to get involved.

That's where I was wrong. Because I kept wondering about that, almost in every conversation I had with other Korean students outside of class, at lunch, or when we met for doing some homework, I always asked them about that. They explained to me that it's not the same not to like politicians than not participating and being informed. Not trusting them has made them watch them and demand more. And they reminded me what they had gone through just before I arrived: they had impeached President Park for a corruption case.

Almost immediately after the news of the President being involved in a corruption case for asking donations in exchange for favors within the government, citizens reacted. There were protests and petitions in the whole country to make her resign or have her removed from office. That was in October. Three months later, she wasn't President anymore. She was removed. She lost her immunity, and she was charged and incarcerated. The Prime Minister stayed in charge. And even being about politics, government, destitutions and new elections, Koreans like for things to happen quickly. For the next month of May, they already had campaigns and elections and the new President was already sworn in.

A clear example for the whole world of how democracy should work. Without tolerating corruption even at the highest level and at the country's most important office. They are doing way better than us. And South Korea became a democracy on the nineties. We have been there for decades. And it doesn't seem to be improving.

Like I told in some other place in this book, in Coahuila, my state, they took five months to solve the case about the governor's election validity. They extended the process until there was one day left for the governor elect to be sworn in. I'm sure they could have done it way before. We have to get used to demand for things to happen. Things well done. And fast.

How many more generations are we going to take to make Mexico one of the best countries in the world?

This trip seems completely different to when I had been in Europe. I compared a lot at first. And it's never good to do it.

In Poland I was with a group of twenty Mexicans. Now I was with a group of a hundred and fifty foreigners from different countries. There I had met young people almost my age who were making history in their country's politics, in Korea they hated it. And if I needed inspiration in Europe, I just had to walk on the street and see the beautiful gardens they had, surrounded by historic and important buildings. It's the old world, after all. Their constructions are sumptuous and luxurious. Like the Louvre museum or Queen Elizabeth's and her family's palaces that seem taken out of a tale. In the palace rooms in Korea, rooms were empty. Instead of having giant libraries or carved wood bookcases, the three or four book the emperor had, were on the floor. Instead of having enormous beds, they just put some pillow on the floor. And instead of having room-sized desks, they just needed a wooden board to put on their crossed legs.

It disappointed me getting to places so important and impressive like the emperor's palace, and discovering that there was nothing interesting nor spectacular inside. We toured all the rooms or palace sections, but everything was empty. And at the museums from different dynasties' belongings that governed Korea, there were only vases and pots.

Several days passed until I made myself stop comparing. If I didn't stop doing it, I wasn't going to enjoy all the summer. I wasn't in Europe, the old world. I was in the new one. If I wanted to understand and learn how they had achieved to be one of the best, I had to open my mind. After I realized I wasn't making the most out of it, I went to the university's calmest place, the library, and I started reflecting. I understood everything little by little.

For centuries, Koreans had lived under the culture of living with this in mind: less, is more. That way of thinking is everywhere. It can even be seen in the city, because, even though the new buildings are impressive, with shapes and designs that seem from the future, there are horrible and identical buildings that are surely from the eighties. We laughed at first saying that they built the first one, they copied it, and pasted it on every block. But they couldn't get distracted at that time. They wanted to be the best. They had to be efficient. The time where they would be able to worry about the appearance of their constructions would come (and they would be some of the best). They couldn't back then.

Now I admire that capacity of concentrating on the important thing. If they have achieved to become what they are now, it's precisely because of that. They have made plans. They have focused on the important. And they kept focused on finishing the steps or stages of that plan.

In one of the UN's General Assembly meetings, in 2013, Malala Yousafzai, Nobel Peace Prize, she gave one of her most famous and emotive speeches. There's where she said this:

"One child, one teacher, one book, one pen can change the world. Education is the only solution".

And that, education, was what changed the world for Koreans. The surprising and fast recovery from war that Korea had from the sixties was thanks to the best investment they made. The best one of their lives. Being a country in extreme poverty, and where almost 80% of its population didn't know how to read or write, they concentrated and bet everything on one thing: education.

In one of the museums I visited, there's a whole area dedicated to that time. There are very aware of the fact that what they have, what they are and all they have achieved, is thanks to that national effort that was made so everyone was prepared to build the future they now live in. Because they had no money, it can be clearly seen in the museum's scale models, the classrooms were on the sidewalks. With seats and desks made out of recycled wooden boxes. But the kids and young people were studying, no matter the facilities, if you could even call them that.

In the nineties, 93% of Koreans already knew how to read and write. And not just that. They started to generalize that there were only two ways for being part of the middle class. Study a professional career and get a degree. Or enroll in a military career for life.

It's very different now. Of course. They are one of the best economies in the world. But they haven't stopped insisting, not even nowadays, on looking to have the best education. Because if not, who would plan the cities, who would take care of the economy, who would be the scientists, who would invent new technologies, who would govern?

Mexico has a big challenge on this topic. It's

exaggeratedly common to hear politicians talk about the urge of improving education. There have been many reforms (and the last one is already being cancelled). But there has been a few progress with all of them. In the measurements from the Organization for Economic Co-operation and Development, we're always in the last place among all the countries.

And at least since I have memory, it's always been known that education in Mexico is very bad. I don't understand why it's still like that. There's no need to reinvent the wheel. We have the example of systems that have worked in other countries. We just need this to be a government's priority.

It would be very different if governments had as a phrase or slogan something that motivated to go farther and have higher study degrees. And campaigns focused on making education also be a citizens' priority. Not like now where all have phrases and campaigns that try to say everything in their government is perfect. Someone still believes that?

Just like Mexico came together after September's earthquake in 2017, Korea has had similar moments throughout its history.

Years ago, when they were still a poor country, the government had a program to help people have their own house. What they did was launch a program to distribute construction material to whoever needed it.

From there, they knew they wouldn't achieve much if they weren't united. And that they would go farther if they united. The people from the same neighborhood all helped one person build their house. When they finished, they got onto the next one. Just like that, until everyone had their house, built in community. That started replicating across the country. Then, the government came back, inspected, and because they had made a good use of the material, they gave them more. Now to build the second story. Again all as a community, they made it.

I have seen in Mexico how trucks arrive to poor neighborhoods to distribute cement packages. It works like this: they park, people arrive and take packages by carrying them, and there's never a formal follow up on the usage they give to that material. And they don't even give it to those who need it most. Rather, they just give them away to ask (buy) for votes, like many more things.

Then the good years came.

After that fast-economic development time, in 1997

there was a crisis in the whole Asian continent. Korea didn't save itself from it. Although they were already a big economy, the crisis was so strong in Asia, that they had to go to the limit of requesting a loan from the International Monetary Fund. So, they already owed money

The government did cuts to public spending, they made an industrial and commercial restructure, they closed businesses and companies that weren't generating what was expected, and promoted new laws to try to adjust the new budget to try to pay the debt they had.

And once again. People from Korea doing their thing.

The citizens, the normal people, promoted a national campaign to help the country pay that credit from the IMF they had requested. Families went out on the streets voluntarily, not to protest. But this time to donate the gold they had. 227 tons were collected. In less than five years they had already finished paying the debt. And they started to grow even more.

These are the values and education Korea has. They're capable of uniting in the problems to face them together. They know that for the future to be good, they have to put effort in this precise moment. And they do it gladly. So many sacrifices, so many work hours, so much dedication, passion and willingness for things to happen and happen fast, have given great results. Like just 16% of the population is in a poverty situation. Compared to the 52% in Mexico.

No country is perfect. There's a huge problem in Korea. One that has repeated across the world.

Countries that have or have had a fast-economic development, or in which they have achieved not to have lack of resources, have seen an increase of social problems.

Unfortunately, Korea is one of the countries with the highest suicide rates. It's a complex problem, but it sums up in social and family pressure. Mostly, in teenagers and senior people.

Anything taken to the extreme is bad. Like I said, for Koreans, personal and family honor is the most valuable thing a person can possess. The pressure is really high. For them, not getting into one of the three best universities in the country is losing or harming the family's honor, reputation and prestige. That's why, since they are kids, they spend about 16 hours daily at school, in classes and extracurricular activities to achieve the preparation needed to get into one of those three best universities. The government even had to pass a law that prohibited paying for private classes outside school, to avoid rich people have a privilege on their kid's preparation.

And it gets worse. When they graduate, they future they have waiting for them depends on the university they graduated from and the grades they got. But it doesn't end there. They are the country that sleeps the least. And the one that works the most.

And when problems like depression, lack of self-esteem arise, and it becomes a serious problem, suicide is the way out they find. If they go with a doctor, a psychologist or some specialist, they think it's also putting in danger the impeccable honor of their family. The government has even tried to stop this problem in different ways. But not even with the best public health systems have they achieved progress.

Most of the buildings have a mesh so they don't try to jump. There are nets beneath stairs and handrails at shopping malls. And the metro stations aren't like in Europe, where there's a line painted on the floor that you have to avoid stepping on not to fall on the rain tracks. In Korea there are doors that open automatically until the train has arrived and the car is completely still.

I can't imagine what I would feel not seeing another way

out than that. In my city, the number of people who decide to end their life has been increasing. And it's something so delicate that as many solutions as you think there are, you can't reach one. It's something so personal, that many times it could happen that the not even the people around someone can realize the problems they are facing.

I wish with all my heart that those who are going through hard problems in their lives, ask for help. And we, on the other hand, have to learn to listen to people. That can change everything.

One afternoon I was walking through an enormous bridge. It crossed a river. The Han River. Anywhere I looked, I saw enormous buildings. Companies. Big constructions. Shopping malls. And thousands of cars and people.

During the different trips I've had, I had realized how small I am in comparison to the world's size. Walking through that bridge I was thinking the same. But with a greater intensity.

I was in the world's biggest city. It was exciting. Also intimidating.

I imagined the millions of people. And where I was I

could see the movement and dynamism of an entire city. Lights from cars going all ways. The metro arriving and leaving again. Its stations with thousands of people waiting to get in. People arriving and walking to their destinations. Lights from elevators in all those buildings going up and down. There should be millions of transactions per second in the thousands of stores in a city like that. People presenting projects. Closing deals. I imagined the number of businessmen, students, professionals, artists, politicians, kids, dads, grandparents, tourists, everyone doing important things.

Seven billion people. Seven billion stories, dreams, ambitions, passions, and goals. And among all the people in the world, there I was. Walking in the middle of a bridge.

In the middle of all that I was seeing and the immense world I was imagining, I was just an insignificant student from another country walking with a backpack with a water bottle, a journal, my phone, and an umbrella.

I started asking myself what was my place in the world. Or if there would really be one for me.

"Can a person really change the world?", I asked myself. The way each one can think about it, the answer will

always be a yes. There are thousands of stories everywhere that prove it. In all those stories, the only thing that has been required is a problem to solve, a cause worth fighting for or a company that needs to be started.

I enjoyed one of the best views in the city for the last time.

More calm. Without any rushes. Without thinking too much. Just enjoying the moment.

When I finished crossing the Han River, I rented a bike and biked by the shore. I stayed reading under Lotte Tower, the fifth tallest in the world. I looked for my favorite books in the most modern library I had ever visited. I bought Harry Potter and the Philosopher's Stone in Korean at a metro station.

I took my last Soju bottle. And I stayed hours looking at the city from the Bongeunsa temple. My favorite place in the whole city. From there you can see the traditional temples in Korea along with the most modern buildings you can imagine. A mixture from the past and the future in a single look.

Those of us who were left went to have dinner for the last time at a Korean BBQ restaurant. And we were talking about the plans each one had and laughing about the things we have lived together.

I took the last pictures of the city. And I convinced myself that Mexico will be a first world country one day.

Like Korea.

RESPONSABILITY

"We don't fear the future.
We shape it."

–

Barack Obama

We Were Would Like to Live

I struggled to concentrate. I was still thinking about the trip. Everyone was fed up. At home, at school, and at work, I was always talking about Korea. And every time I ran into someone, the only thing I wanted to do was to stop the conversation, take my phone out, and show them the pictures of the city I had taken. I took very personal the mission of making everyone realize the city and country we could have.

I arrived with a lot of ideas at work, but I realized there were only five months left until the time was over for the Mayor to be my boss. Maybe not much was left to be done. How fast had it gone by? It was a good time to start seeing what had been accomplished and what was missing. And make the last effort to leave good results.

At that moment, the city had already been recognized as the second best to live in. And the fourth safest in the country. Many thought we had bought these awards to brag that the government had done something good. No! The truth is we found out about those awards and recognitions thanks to the news. But the opposition managed to spread many fake news, that sometimes were impossible to counter.

In the end, with the experience he had, the Mayor had a clearer and wider idea of what had to be done in a city to make it move forward the best way. And he wanted to be in charge, from his office Congress, of creating laws so that cities were required to have a finance plan, control systems, and a long-term plan. He also wanted to make sure all the cities in the country were getting the budget they should get. In a few words, he was ready to become a federal deputy.

I wasn't going to support someone who didn't deserve it. I admire and respect him. That's why when he told us he was going to run for office, I went all-in. There was a lot to do. Mostly, with the strategy and digital innovation part. My strength.

I didn't feel sad when his administration ended. Because I didn't have time to be. Instead of resting all December, like I had planned because my job was over, and because I was on vacation from school, I spent it working on the campaign. There was still a lot of time before it started (months). But the ideas were many. And when I'm passionate about something, there's no one who can stop me. I redesigned his website. Finished, and started to design the new strategy. Detail by detail.

Truth being told, we got to do many things that haven't been done before. Every time someone commented on Twitter or Facebook about how we were doing the best campaigns I felt extremely proud of my work.

We went out to the city center, to restaurants, or shopping malls, and people approached him. Most people took a photo with him or thanked him for what he had done for the city. You could feel people's love. And I wanted everyone to have the chance to listen to him and spend time talking to him, in person. And that led us to do one of the things that made his campaign different.

Many of the campaigns from typical politicians, are about making enormous events with big crowds, give things away and promise things they will never do. But there's never a real contact between those candidates and the people they want to represent.

We opened a space on the former Mayor's website so that anyone could choose the date and time that was more convenient for them to go have a coffee with him. And it was a huge success. We had to open more dates every time. There were even three or four per week. I loved it because everything was organized online thanks to that app on his website. Those who registered got automatic reminders, and links to confirm their attendance. At the beginning I didn't know if it was going to work. Many click the "confirm" button online at events, even though they know they aren't going. But it worked since the first time we did it.

There was just one rule: say whatever they were thinking. They could complain, propose, give their opinion or whatever they wanted. It was totally casual and open. That made them feel like they were among friends. And they told us they didn't know if it was true that he was going to be there. And it impressed them even more that three or four hours could go by, and that, even though his team was telling him he had to go somewhere else, he stayed there. Listening to the stories and problems of each one of them.

I sat at another table and listened with detail to what the people who went to those coffee meetings talked about. I didn't know about any other politician who was spending time paying real attention to real problems from people. Something that should be normal at any government level. And in any representation-based democracy.

If it was eleven at night already, the coffee shop employees started giving us signals that they had to close. When everyone said goodbye and went to their homes, even though it was really late, I felt cheered and full of energy after so many proposals that came out of those talks. Other times, the stories they told were heartbreaking.

I stayed thinking all night about how they achieved to keep going after what had happened to them. Sometimes I couldn't come up with solutions. Those were the sad days of the campaign. At least for me.

I have a journal full of notes about those problems. I check them every now and then. They're so many. But as hard and tough as some may seem, I know solutions can be found. The only thing needed is someone who listens to the people. Someone who believes in them. And fights for them.

I knew I wasn't going to be the federal deputy. But at the same time I understood that having the opportunity of advising and being close to someone who would have the responsibility of proposing and changing the country's laws, was the closest I had been to generating a change. A big one. I set myself the objective to be more proactive than before.

A campaign is also about sharing the vision. Mostly, you have to demonstrate you have the capacity to make it real.

Even though my job was to design the digital strategy, I wanted to give an extra trying to design and write the vision Isidro had outlined during almost four years. And not just considering what he wanted for the state or the country, but also what most of the people thought it was urgent to solve. Because we dream daily with a better country. One where we can live in peace. One where politicians don't steal. One where the government isn't corrupt. And one where everyone who puts effort and follows the game rules does well.

Regardless of those who think we will achieve it one day, or those who don't, we would all like for it to happen.

But what exactly?

The dream we all have is a little ambiguous. Not too specific. We don't have a plan for how to get to it. Because, although in our imagination, that Mexico is perfect in general, we don't have it clear how it would be on the particular.

What laws would there be? Would they be obeyed? What taxes would be payed? How would the politician's acts would be? What would be the problems to face? How involved would the citizens and the private sector be?

In the companies there's a general director or a CEO. His job is to set out the vision and make it happen. No company can achieve to reach its goals if they don't have them established.

IN the case of government, now they publish an expense document called National, State, or City Development Plan, depending on the government's level. But I have never seen them mention it again after they announce it. It even seems a checklist all politicians do when they are sworn in:

1 Make forums and events to collect proposals (or pretend they do).

2 Publish the development plan.

3 Announce at every place and media as a big accomplishment.

4 Forget about it and never look to have the results that were planned.

Going back to the comparison, at the companies, the CEO responds to the board or the stakeholders. Besides having a vision, there has to be a strategic planning and control systems to be able to measure the results. It would be unthinkable for a company to be changing its director every six years, each one of them with totally different intentions. Cutting off the land from the last director and starting from scratch. But when it comes to government it even seems normal. Change of administration. Change of employees. Change of government plans. Change of everything.

Ok. Changes are always good. Yes, when they are strategic. Not when they're pulled out of the sleeve to demonstrate a new government has just entered.

Since 2017 I was thinking about launching an organization dedicated to promote law initiatives and young citizen candidacies. It was going to be called *Mexico Posible*. We even had the website designed. But it stayed there. Just in plans. In 2018 Salvador Alva published a book with that same name (not a complaint). It was a great personal lesson that the world is of those who do things, not those who says and plans them infinitely.

Salvador's book is now one of my favorites. I have recommended it to my friends, acquaintances and to some of my representatives over Twitter. Hopefully it was a mandatory read for everyone in public office. And for every citizen.

With direct and precise words, Salvador explains how a country has to have a vision that we all share. Governors and politicians, the private sector, and citizens. And we all have to be focused on making it a reality. Just like at the best companies.

Salvador explains that a vision reveals what the organization's purpose is and what it wishes to accomplish on a short term. And that they're words that can have a big strength. If they are well made, of course. There are studies which demonstrate that employees who found value and meaning in their organization's vision develop nineteen percent more commitment than in organizations where there is none or it isn't energetic.

It preferably has to be short. And it has to convey the passion of its founders and the purpose the organization seeks to achieve.

For example, Disney's vision is simple: "Make people happy". Ted conferences' vision: "Spread ideas". Google's: "Organize the world's information and make it universally accessible and useful".

What happens when that vision isn't there in an organization: "The debate centers in judging, blaming, lowering the self-esteem, feed pessimism, and divide its inhabitants". It sounds very familiar to what's happening in the country.

Because Isidro is a businessman, he already knew those topics. He always told us how important it is to have a vision, a plan, and everything that Salvador explains in his book. But I think he could never transmit the idea or the clear explanation to get all the team to understand him. At the meetings, when he started talking about this, it gave me the impression that all the city's area directors thought that was just for companies. And that there were so many things to do in the government, that they couldn't lose the time to stop and define a powerful vision that got to move and transform the whole city.

That's the flaw in governments. They work like different organizations. And they don't achieve to be effective or efficient.

There are countries that have been working on that. In an article, Jörgen Eriksson made a collection of the most significant visions some countries have set. Like Malaysia. In 1997 they establish the vision to be a completely developed country by 2020. At the same time, Singapore set the vision to become a global city-state, by 2021. And the city of Abu Dhabi in 2009 set the vision to establish a system to align all the public policies and plans that contribute to the economic development of the Emirates in a single axis by 2030.

In the Global Competitiveness Report 2017-2018 Malaysia positioned itself as the 23rd most competitive economy in the world. Singapore's economy has already been recognized the most open in the world, the seventh least corrupt and the most ideal to do business. And Abu Dhabi already represents one-third of the United Arab Emirates economy.

These are the examples from vision and results we need. That vision has to excite us with its own energy. It has to be doable. Realistic. But also challenging. All Mexico has to know it. And when that happens, we will all be able to start making decisions based on that. Every local or federal administration has to also take it as a base. At this moment each of the thirty-two states in Mexico is going different ways. And what to say about the cities inside the states. Two thousand and four hundred municipalities. All of them on their own path.

There's a tale we all know. Maybe because of the book, the animated movie or the live-action film. This is one of the dialogues (between the smiling cat and a girl):

- "Could you please tell me which path should I take to get out of here?", Alicia said.

- "That depends on where you want to go."

- "It doesn't matter where", she replied.

- "Then it really doesn't matter which path you take."

- "I just want to get somewhere."

- "I assure you that if you walk enough by any road you will get somewhere", the cat said.

Regardless if we do something or not, or regardless if we choose one path or the other, we're going to get somewhere. That applies for people, organizations, and for institutions. As much as for companies and governments.

Let's stop taking paths we don't know where they will

get us or that make us lose time. Like the author and filmmaker Joel Barker said, vision without action is just a dream. Action without vision is losing time. And vision with action is what makes the difference.

When NAFTA was established between Mexico, US, and Canada, it went well. Jobs came. There was foreign investment like never before. And we started to have an economical recovery. We stopped being an agricultural country and we achieved to become a manufacturing one. But the economical recovery wasn't the one we had hoped for. In many economic reports, analysts agree that, since the nineties, our laws need to be reformed to take advantage of that development there was, achieve that it became exponential and that everyone did better.

Three decades later, and we're practically still in the same conditions. It still is the same manufacturing country we started to be in the nineties. And multinational companies are the ones who still dominate the market and create value.

But it is what it is. Now what we have to do is define the action we will take to improve this.

It has already been more than twenty years since Mexico opened to the world. Since then I don't understand what has been happening that makes things not happen to make the most out of our potential. Has it happened to you that you feel frustrated thinking that Mexico has everything it needs to be successful, unlike other countries that don't have anything and are doing better? It has happened to me. Many times. We have to convert that frustration that you, and the majority of Mexicans feel, into specific actions. And demands.

In regard to being more specific about the kind of country we all want, Salvador Alba also presents an analysis about what the best rated countries in the world have in common. I like it because in between so many problems the country has, those four points are a good place to start. And they are like a practical guide of where we have to get.

The best countries focus on attraction and formation of talent, without a socio-economical distinction. They have digital governments, with open and effective institutions that promote research and entrepreneurship. And their cities are fun and safe to live in, with a high level of urban concentration based on a vertical growth.

That's it. We don't have to keep losing time any longer. Or try to reinvent the wheel. Let's focus on achieving that in Mexico.

First, what I see is that governments, through their economical development secretaries from each state or city, have clung to get foreign companies to arrive and invest. Not because those companies are going to increase people's quality of life. More so, they do it because the government's goal is to announce numbers on new jobs. And they spend millions of pesos on putting up ads with those numbers. I think that if people do better and they start having better opportunities, they will realize it. There's no need to spend so much money from our taxes on advertisement.

Coahuila is a clear example of this. There's a work rotational rate from 60%. Employees change companies for a raise of even twenty pesos. But the state's government is still looking for foreign manufacturing companies to arrive and install in the state. Making the problem even bigger. Because companies that arrive don't look for engineers, graduates, or specialists. What they look for is people that will do technical, predefined, and repetitive tasks. The local market saturated with this type of jobs.

The next stage, for Coahuila, any state, and the entire country: attraction and formation of talent. Any student that demonstrates potential and talent, shouldn't struggle to keep doing it. On the contrary. Doors for new and better opportunities should be opened for them.

Thinking about boys and girls who love to go school but are forced, by their parents and the situations they are going through, o quit their studies, makes me think how bad we are. The worst thing is that there are not just a few students who go through that. Every year there are more than a million kids and teenagers that have to do it. And it becomes something repetitive. How are they supposed to overcome everything when they had to abandon what was going to give them impulse?

More and better schools are urgent. But not just that. Also having a meritocracy system that can detect talent. From every type: academic, sports, creative and artistic, leadership and entrepreneurial. There has to be a support for them so they can develop their knowledge and ability even more.

And among many foreign companies that have arrived to Mexico, how many will be universities? None. The government is just seeking to announce job numbers. A good way to promote a higher education level, besides a meritocratic system, is to bring universities and students from other countries. And that Mexicans study abroad with the commitment of retuning to help us lead the change and improve things with everything they learned.

It's proven that many times we can't aspire to become something, if we can't see it. When the campaigns started in 2017 and Enrique Peña Nieto proposed to create several trains, I thought it was something old fashioned. Something that would make us go back. I imagined an outdated type of transport that no one would use. But of course, after going to Europe and Asia I have a totally different idea about public transport. Trains in Mexico are urgent! But I didn't realize that until I used them myself. That's why it's important that Mexican students have opportunities in other countries. So, they can see everything we can become.

I have a lot to say about digital governments. In my company I have been able to help other companies and institutions make their processes digital and be more efficient. So, I have some experience on that.

The only thing I had to do was open my computer every time a new semester started, get into my university's website, login with my username and password, select my schedule and save it. Then generate my registration, and that's it! I was enrolled within minutes. I love it because any process I had to do in my university, was already digital. I didn't have to do much than just several clicks. If I had a question or wanted to communicate with someone, I looked for their email in their directory. I wrote them. And they replied. Only a few times I had to go in person besides for class.

As an entrepreneur, professional, and citizen, I have had to do many government processes. Of every kind. They are like a reminder of how far behind we are. In the majority of the government's offices they still ask for receipts, copies, originals, hand written documents. Many of the things they ask for have no sense. They keep the printed documents? They scan them? They take it to the computer? Or where do so many things go? They haven't understood that we rare in the twenty-first century. And it's not like we just discovered the internet.

There are Mexican companies that are also doing it extremely well. There's Cinepolis' case. You can buy your tickets and select your seats from an app. Now you can even add popcorn and soda from the app so you don't have to line up at the cafeteria. And that's while you accumulate points on your frequent client card. That you can use to pay what you want or rent a movie in Klick. They have taken years to achieve this. But my respects go out for them. Because you can tell what they want is their clients to have the best experience.

And who doesn't like to order pizza online? Or pay your phone's bill? Or whatever it is, as long as it is online?

And if a Mexican movie theater chain is looking to daily innovate and make their customers spend less time at the ticket window and more time doing everything on their app, why isn't the Mexican government doing that? They are supposed to have more budget. More personnel. More capacity. Now we need that anyone can do it over their home. On their phone or computer.

Digitalize and make processes more efficient is going to help a lot on making them transparent. Because you can establish indicators that update in real time and publicly present them. Imagine all the purchases and government accounts available the same time the movements were made.

Each one going their own was isn't going to work. We are already watching that. We have to make universities, companies, and research centers increase in quality and quantity, but also to link them. Generating innovations of all kind. And the importance of all of them being linked is do that they can generate ideas and actions that are needed in the market and the industry. Working together to achieve it. Because it doesn't serve a purpose to create something new if no one needs or requires it.

And, lastly, fun and safe cities. I loved that definition. Because it involves the recreational spaces, the activities everyone can calmly do, and the safety and peace environment we would like to have.

In Japan and Korea, I could feel calm about leaving my computer open and my backpack on a desk while I had to go to the restroom or ask for another cup of green tea. And I also saw how kids ten or twelve years old went to school walking by themselves or in groups of more kids. Without adults watching over them.

Not having the worry of someone stealing your things or not having to think about the possible dangers, makes people concentrate in other important things. We only have one brain. We can't think of many things at once. The safety of a country and any individual is part of the Maslow's pyramid. If we cross that out and we mark it as done, it's going to let us keep going to the construction of a better economy and society.

I was sure that, from Congress, Isidro would promote all of this. At the middle of the campaign, I was so excited that I did a presentation about these ideas. And I insisted that he had to read Salvador Alva's book as soon as possible. They were the same ideas he had. But better explained.

The government isn't a company. But it is the biggest organization in the country. And probably under any corporate standard, it would already be broke and would have disappeared years ago. It has a big debt. People don't trust it. It doesn't respond to the current needs. And it's exaggeratedly outdated.

The book series "The Accursed Kings" tells the story of the French monarchy starting in 1314. I love them. They're written by Maurice Druon. And Maurice has something, that could tell historic facts in a way that you feel part of that time. In the third book of the series, when Felipe the Handsome's son, Luis X, has just been crowned as king, I found this quote about what it means to govern (in which Luis X was terrible at):

> *"From all human activities, governing others, even being the most envied, is the most disappointing one, because it never*

has an end and it doesn't allow any rest
for the spirit. The baker who has taken out
his batch, the woodcutter in front of cut
wood, the judge who just ordered an
arrest, the architect who sees a finished
building, the painter once finished his
work, can, at least for one night, enjoy that
relative tranquility that a finalized effort
produces. The governor, never. A political
difficult seems to ease when another, while
the first was being solved, demands
immediate attention."

It's complicated. That's why we need dynamic governors. Who are focused on solving problems. Who have the capacity to gather the best team. Who work with a vision, a plan, and a strategic plan for a long term.

We can't keep demanding this to someone who simply doesn't have the capacity or interest to do it. There are profiles for everything. There's the importance of citizens choosing well who is going to represent us. Each election has to be like a job interview. Candidates present their CV. We research them. We verify they comply with the abilities and capacities needed to fulfill the position they are applying for. And after that, we vote for them.

If you have understood to perfection this whole chapter,

or if you had heard before about what needs to be done and you agree on this country's vision, you can be part of the people who help to give it an impulse!

To anyone who's reading this book: if money is what interests you, governing for power, or governing to have recognition, to be a leader and get to do things your way, then it's better that you never consider running for public office. There's not going to be support.

But if you're passionate about working for your community, anywhere, and you also like planning, decision making, conflict resolution, reuniting and listening to people, making diagnosis, you're the kind of person the country needs! Consider, please, at some point in your life (the sooner the better) running for public office. You can't imagine the big change you can make. And the amount of people who will support you.

A big part of the problem is that we don't believe in politics and government. And that makes the best profiles get away from wanting to be a part of this. The idea that politics isn't for decent people is very stuck in our heads. And with reason. We have been through everything. And a lot of people have walked in to the government and done everything. Well, there's no other way. Decent people from the country have to get in. And by decent people I mean the honest ones. The ones with an open mind. The ones who want to gather the best team. Even better profiles than theirs. And make the best decisions together.

Since we're in school, since high school and universities, in class and extracurricular activities, you can see the different personalities of people. And everywhere I've seen those students identified as "the future politicians". Surely you have seen them too. For what I have seen, normally those people have the ease of speaking, diction and presence, they give good speeches, they are involved with different causes and they will always be the group's voice. And I have no doubt that many of them will give excellent results if they decide to continue that way. But maybe it's time to leave those future politicians' stereotypes aside. Let's look more into the capacities. We all like to talk to someone who is incredibly charismatic. They give us energy. But we have to balance things out. We can't afford to make decisions based on someone's perception anymore. We have to go deeper.

When we see the most dedicated, the most involved, not necessarily the most charismatic, but those who like to get into details, those who want to solve problems, those who listen to different opinions, who ask for advice, and those who want to charge thing in an ordered and organized way, those are the ones we have to give impulse to be the next politicians and governors.

There's an enormous amount of money they give to parties and that parties give to candidates. That money comes from our taxes. Directly. And whatever they do, they will have it. There, starts one of the biggest problems we have.

In the elections and campaigns I have seen, I have been able to prove it again and again. Both the party and the candidate make the minimum effort to get real citizen support during their political careers. And I haven't seen anyone who actually worries about having a real and constant communication with the people who chose them. Giving explanations. Yes. But also opening spaces for dialogue.

But they don't try. Because parties, one way or another, will receive the money they were assigned. We only have to remember how the last presidential campaigns were. Not worthy at all from the position they were seeking. They danced on stages and stood on podiums without a speech. They said whatever occurred to them. Like some opinion leaders say, we are in the *worstcracy*. We have to choose the least worst among the worse.

There's no perfect democracy in the world. Even though there are some better than others. They're all a continuous improvement process. And not because things are like they are now, it means they have to stay like that forever and that in the future any action has to be under the current rules.

One of the things I'm the most certain about: there's another way to do it. There's another Mexico we can get to have.

What we have to do is create a dynamic electoral ecosystem where anyone can run for public office. And the play field has to be even for everyone. What happened to Margarita Zavala, Jaime Rodríguez, Pedro Ferriz and other people who want to be independent candidates can't happen again. Anyone who is sure they can do a good job representing us, should have the doors totally open. If they decide to be independent, perfect. And if they wanted to run through a part, they should also have the doors open. All with the same chance of winning.

If anyone wanted to run at this moment, they would start with a bank account in ceros, competing against someone who has millions of pesos. The solution isn't to give the independent candidate the same amount of money than to a party's candidate. Mi idea is to take the money away and the free TV or radio ads. To any kind of candidate. And to every party.

There's the initiative "Without vote, there is no money", in which it's proposed that parties only get the proportional percentage of money to the amount of people who vote in every election. We have to be tougher: zero budget.

To win, a candidate would have to get the real support from people. And their campaign would have to hire the best team possible to be able to communicate everything they want to do if they are elected in an innovative way. They would have to get donations. Use all the digital tools. Recruit volunteers. Knock doors. Build databases. They would need to have the best strategy and the best proposals. That is, wining thanks to people. Making enough efforts. Demonstrating with facts how their government would be. Being consistent. Updating themselves. Studying topics and problems. Preparing speeches with the policies they would implement.

If I saw a candidate that is not so well known, but

convinces me with proposals, I get identified with them, and I feel I can trust they will do a great work, I would love to donate twenty or fifty pesos to their campaign to help them convince more people. The more people they convince and believe in their project, the more donations they will get.

When I say that about every party and candidate having to look for donations to finance themselves, they always tell me it is a danger. That the money from organized crime would end in the campaigns. The truth is they already do. So what we have to do is that, by law, any transaction a party and a candidate makes in campaign, has to be registered and showed in a web portal. If they have done it in other countries, why not us?

It can be achieved to make parties transparent and take the public money away from them. We just need to keep debating on how. But in a rush. If not, we will take fifty years more before it happens.

I have already been watching over a polling station. Every time parties make alliances it becomes a disaster to count votes. The amount of water paper is impressive. And many people don't even know who they are voting for. They let themselves be guided by the party. And if there are elections for president, governor, deputies, and senators, four different sheets of paper are handed. Again: not because ballots have always been like that, it means that they have to keep being like that for the rest of our lives.

We can vote with one single ballot. One that is divided in two, three, four or five. Depending on how many positions are being chosen. And without colors and logos. In black and white. We just need the name of the candidate, what they are running for, and a box or circle to be able to vote for that person. That's it. With that we would end with many of the country's illnesses. It would be a step forward for having a culture in which we vote for the person, not for a party.

Those are some of the electoral topics. And some ideas. But what we have to do is take all the problems the country has, check how they're trying to get solved, and look for new solutions. Goodbye to the old ideas. We have to innovate and keep a continuous improvement culture. Yes, even in the government (mostly in the government!).

"We cannot build our own future without helping others to build theirs."

–

Bill Clinton

Returns Are Accepted

We hadn't talked about it. But I was expecting that once Isidro had won the election, he would invite me to be a part of his team. And if that didn't happen, I was going to propose it myself. I had some reforms in mind, proposals and some projects. I even started putting up a file with the topics I thought were urgent.

In my head, there was always the idea of getting to the elected deputy's house just the next day after the election with a big file. And start looking and studying those topics deeply and having a brainstorm session and day-long debates to find the best solutions.

Each sheet on that file had already the letterhead with the Congress' logo. I took it very seriously. There was even a section where I put, structured in a flow chart, how the office's service and communication was going to be with the people from the district. I wanted him to be the closest and accessible deputy in the country.

We were sure he was going to win. On the surveys we had, he was ahead. We had made a different campaign. And it was evident everywhere. There were financial problems in the middle of the campaign. But him and the team that was left still did everything that was possible.

But he didn't win. It was like one of those lessons life gives you where something or someone superior to you tries to tell you not everything will go as you want. That, even if it's good to plan and have goals, it's also good to have a Plan B. I didn't have it.

I still thought he was going to win the same day of the election. At midnight, when we finished counting the votes from my station, I already knew he had lost. I was totally exhausted after the almost sixteen hours I was making sure people's votes were respected. When I got home, I didn't want anyone to ask me what had happened. I went straight to bed. And I remember perfectly that I had a really vivid dream where Isidro won the election. And we were celebrating. At least I had that nice memory from the dream.

The day after the election I had a trip with all my family. I had to wake up at five in the morning and get into a little truck my grandfather rented to go all together. Everyone was asking me what had happened. But I didn't even know. I turned on do not disturb on my phone. I put my headphones on. I played the music I had downloaded. And I disconnected from everything and everyone.

I couldn't avoid it. There were a lot of thoughts in my head. What did we do well and what did we do wrong? Everything happened so fast. There were moments where I doubted my work. But I did an effort to see things from a broader perspective. And I was sure about something. That dream was already over. I had to focus my energy on what was next.

It's unfair that we don't give a chance to the people with the will to do things right in the government. I saw it closely. Isidro would have been one of the best deputies in Mexico. He had already been recognized as one of the best Mayors in the country. And I'm sure Pedro Kumamoto would have been one of the best senators. But he also lost.

I felt disappointed on the country. Maybe we do have the politicians we deserve, like many say.

These two examples discourage anyone who has a little intention of participating in politics. What's the point? In the end the one the system wants always wins.

I had to accept the results. People voted. That's how a democracy works. But being honest, I don't feel represented in the executive power, nor in the legislative, much less in the judicial one.

The person who won that office, that we lost, did it with a little over 30% of the total votes. Which means the majority didn't choose her. It's strange for that to happen. But it's very common in Mexico. This creates a lot of division. And precisely the sensation that you're not well represented. Besides, it gets hard for everyone. Imagine being a mayor, a deputy, or a President, like Enrique Peña Nieto, with 60% or 70% of the people against you. That's why it was something historic and unique that Andrés Manuel won with more than half. Something that should start to be normal.

I arrived at the hotel and just when I got off the little truck, I found one of my best friends and her family at the entrance. I toured the hotel. I saw the pool and the beach. I normally don't like being under the sun. Now I needed it.

I had been waiting to take those vacations like a little

break before starting all the job we would have in the Congress. Instead of that I was trying to disconnect. I didn't want to know absolutely anything about politics or government.

I turned my phone off. Just enjoy. Don't think much. Take the sun. Walk on the beach. Eat well. Read the books you have.

That's what I did. And it was amazing. After many of months of stress, I felt completely liberated. If several days or weeks before that I would have wanted to turn my phone off, the campaign's team would have gone mad immediately. I had to be available twenty-four seven, checking notifications, messages, and news.

That week was like a chapter closure and the beginning of a new one.

I had two books with me. "1984", George Orwell's dystopia. Ok. Actually, it wasn't a good idea to read "1984" just after the elections. A world in which information is controlled and citizens are watched? No, thank you. I had had much of that in real life. Anyway, I finished reading it, trying not to compare it to what had happened.

In my luggage I also carried a book that I found by

coincidence at the supermarket before I felt. I couldn't leave it there after seeing its title: "Healthy intestine, healthy life". Trying to do many things and projects at once, I always had stomach problems. Because of stress.

I didn't want to think a lot about my Plan B during those days. For the first time in my life, I just enjoyed the moment.

In the hotel, they had a gym, yoga classes and one of the most equipped and big spas I've seen. One day I exercised. The next day I went to yoga. When the class ended the instructor recommended me to go to the spa for a hydrotherapy session. I went into boiling water and then water with ice. Several times. When I came back from vacation, the first thing I did was look for a place to keep practicing yoga. I never fail to go to my classes (almost never). I love that before starting the daily practice, we breathe, sing the mantra and dedicate all our effort and energy to a cause or a person. In the end we rub our hands to generate warmth and we put them on our shoulders, and on the chest, to feel the warmth while we full ourselves with admiration and recognition for that day's work.

Since I practice yoga, I keep focused on what I have to do. I also have affection for it because I started practicing right at the moment I needed it the most.

Doing yoga, meditating and not being stressed, made me see things from another perspective. It's not about my problems. But about everyone's problems.

Not winning that campaign was disappointing and discouraging. I really don't consider it a personal failure. I didn't have the responsibility of controlling and leading the whole campaign. I wasn't the candidate. But it was a big professional failure. Six months of intense work, plus four years being the mayor, all for nothing.

If I think about the problems from all the people we listened to during that campaign, that failure is nothing. Isidro is going to be fine. He has his company. His family. And his hobbies. After all, he wasn't a politician before becoming mayor. It wasn't in his plans. And even though I didn't have a plan B, I realized after those vacations that I wasn't going to be fine too. I had a semester left to finish my career. One small company to make grow. And many abandoned personal projects. But what was going to happen with all the problems from the people we listened to during those six months and that we were hoping to solve?

All the circumstances have brought me where I am

today. Thanks to God, life, mi effort, and my family's. I do have my problems. But they are nothing compared to those the majority of the country is going through. Like not having something to eat. Or not having a house to live in.

If I wanted to remember more problems, I only had to remember the last trips from the campaign. They were in the farthest places from the city. Where after one house there's practically nothing more. Some were made out of blocks or cement. Some seemed made out of wooden boxes and cloths, on slopes that ended in streams. Every time we visited a community on those conditions I started thinking a lot. How many politicians would have been to those same places, with that same people, and had promised them everything was going to change? How many times have they went to vote for someone thinking they would support them this time?

We had met people who were going through a disease, but they had no money or insurance to pay for the urgent medical treatment. And many single moms without finding a job, with a son with a disability at home. We saw kinds on the street, abandoned elders, we listened stories about robberies, frauds, and all the bad things you can imagine.

It's frustrating that politicians and governors don't do anything. But it's even more frustrating that we don't do anything, us the citizens. You and I.

When it's about making efforts to change Mexico, in many conversations a question arises: why? Not in the sense of why it's needed. That's evident with all the problems there are. It's more in the sense of why to get involved. Each one of us is very busy doing our thing. Studying, working, taking care of kids, launching companies... Why, also, would we have to participate to have the country we want? Is it not enough to pay my taxes and vote?

It depends on how each one sees it. To me, participating is like giving back all the good that has happened to me in my life.

As a Tec student, I had the opportunity of listening and meeting David Noel Ramírez in person. Someone really loved inside my university's community. But also, a really admired person. Every time I think about him I find inspiration to keep going.

More than 50 years ago, when he was young and about to go to college, he sent all his paperwork to the Tec to apply for a scholarship. Time went by and they didn't reply to him. Without patience and a will to achieve his dreams, he took a bus from San Juan de Los Lagos to Monterrey. At a counter, they gave him the news that his scholarship request hadn't been approved. Because he didn't have money to go back, he had just one thing to do: insist. He asked to be hosted at a church. And he came back several times to the Tec to look for the person in charge of the scholarships. He even discovers which one was his car and waited for him sitting on a tree to be able to insist! He resisted all the negatives. He kept persisting until the scholarship director told him: "I'm sick of you. Only because you're stubborn, I'm going to give you the scholarship". I can't imagine what he felt when they said that to him. What do you do? Jump, cry, laugh?

To finish cover money from expenses, when he had already achieved to be a Tec student, he asked for a job at the campus' cafeteria in the morning, and at the library at night. That was a will to study. A good one.

He then became the rector of that same university.

David Noel is a person son honorable, that when the electoral time to choose Nuevo Leon's next governor, there was a whole movement online called "A Rector Governor". In social media there was a video showing different parts of speeches he has given thought his life. The movement became so big that David Noel had to publicly accept he was going to take a time to reflect and think about it. After a few days he declared he wasn't going to participate as a candidate. Because he was going to continue transforming lives through education.

To us he was, and still is, a public figure. He's like a rockstar. Mostly, after he became famous among Tec students in the country with a meme where he appears talking in the front of a classroom and pointing his head towards a student's head, with the text "receive the entrepreneurial lightning". It went viral. After that, every time someone saw him, they asked him for a picture with the pose sending the famous entrepreneurial lightning.

Every time he can, David Noel reminds us in his speeches we have to pay our social mortgage. It's his favorite topic. And I don't blame him. On the contrary. I thank him for every opportunity he has to remind us. Because we all have that mortgage. We have to pay it sooner or later.

Millions of factors and variables in the universe aligned perfectly to bring us here and now. In the movie "The Butterfly Effect", they explain really well how any minimal detail can change the direction of history. There, the characters travel to the past, they step on a butterfly that shouldn't have been stepped on, and when they came back to the present, reality was completely different. So, imagine the thousands of actions that brought you where you are today.

Even though throughout your life not everything has gone like you expected, I bet you that you are one of the luckiest and most privileged people in the world simply because of the fact that you can dedicate some of your time to read this book. In a country like Mexico, 25 million Mexicans have no access to reading. And 53% of Mexican homes don't have an internet connection in their houses. Even though it's the twenty-first century.

Imagine the number of things you would miss and how hard your life would be if you didn't have access to the internet in your computer or phone. Well, it gets much harder when you have nothing to eat nor a place to live in. We're prone to forget the fact that 43% of the population in Mexico is in a poverty situation.

In talks, discussions and debates I have heard the statement "poor people are poor because they want to", and the other very common one "The one who wants, can". Well, it's one of the most erroneous statements I have heard.

Maslow's pyramid shows the factors that move us closer to a full life. On the base of the pyramid there are the physiological needs, like breathing and food. After comes the second level with is security, both of resources and employment, health, and private property. The third level is the feeling of affiliation, the need to have friendships and receive affection. The fourth level is recognition, trust, and respect. And, finally, the fifth level of the pyramid is self-fulfillment. There a person can be creative, focus on the resolution of problems and understand and accept the facts.

Mexico is still stuck on the first level of that pyramid. There are nine million people in extreme poverty. Meaning, they don't have money to buy something to eat. Someone who has several days without tasting healthy food, without having a house to sleep in or a decent room, how is it supposed for them to aspire to have a better life? They simply have to dedicate themselves to the day to day matters in order to survive.

That's the really serious situation we are in as a country.

What's left to each one of us is recognize the way we

were privileged. Start taking a deep breath. Examine in your mind how your day to day is like. Think about the things you take for granted. Remember the opportunities you have had throughout your life, even if you took them or not. Remember the toughest decisions you had to make. What blessings have you received?

Are you studying? Do you have a job? Do you live in a city? Have you traveled somewhere? Can you go out to a restaurant to have dinner with your friends? Have you started a company? Do you have a hose you can call home? If one of the answers to those questions was a yes, you're already on the other side. You have officially been privileged.

I know that to be where you are, you have had to put on a lot of effort. If not, ask me. What I have done has been based on a lot of dedication. But really, thousands and millions of variables aligned, including your effort and dedication, for your life to be like it is now.

The social mortgage is about realizing where you're standing, and recognizing that millions, literally millions of people, wished with all their heart to be where you are. And it's also about serving others. Not serving ourselves.

Each and every one of us have the power to make the

most out of our situation to start generating a greater good. From the position that you're in. The way that you consider it correct. Just like David Noel. He didn't forget how good life was with him. And now he gives back all the good society has given him, with education.

A while ago I read about the Tec's scholarship program called *"Tomorrow's Leaders"*. They support 100% of the expenses of anyone, without caring where they come from, who demonstrates what they want is to study and lead the change to generate a good.

Those scholarships change lives. Just like over more than 50 years ago changed David Noel's.

Sometimes I imagine the families of the students getting the news about their kids being given a scholarship. It's like saying you won the lottery. And news really full of hope. Like no other. In families that never imagined, due to their economic situation, that their son or daughter would get into one of the best universities in the country.

And one of the things that keeps me full of hope is when I hear the Leaders of Tomorrow, those who got the scholarship, say that when they have the economical possibility, when they graduate and have the job or the company of their dreams, they will donate and support that same program's fund, so more people like them, in any situation that they're in, have the same opportunity they are having. The best example of someone aware of their social mortgage.

They can't do it alone. The country needs that them and millions of Mexicans more, become committed this way. And aware of what life and society has given them. To start giving it back.

In the own words of David Noel, the social mortgage "is not about giving out a paycheck, but it's about changing our attitude and our lifestyle. It's not giving spare change, but committing ourselves, getting really involved on the social projects from our community. It's defeating the apathy, individualism, materialism, hedonism, and egoism".

Paying our social mortgage, is the only way to achieve advancing on the topics that concern us. Any way you see it, in the end, there's a benefit for everyone. The more people that do well, the better the conditions we're going to have as a community.

The country would completely transform itself completely if for example 20% of the people who have had the privilege and opportunity to study a professional career, looked for a way to make the other 80% of Mexicans, who haven't had it, also have the way of getting a degree. And yet better, if 56% of Mexicans who aren't in a poverty situation, looked for the way to help the other 43% get out of it. Just like in Korea where the citizens helped everyone build their house. One by one.

I want to think that the Social Development Secretary or the Economy Secretary checks daily on the problems and urgent topics. And that they are developing strategies and new ideas on how to combat poverty and the educational delay we have. But even if they are doing it or not, what they have done hasn't worked.

We can't keep waiting. We have to go in ourselves to fix the problem. We have to demonstrate that we do understand that for our country to do well, everyone has to do well!

In an agricultural country like ours, there shouldn't be food problems. From my point of view, that topic is the most urgent one. Make sure that no one lacks something to eat. Once that is solved, we could start seeing what's next.

But we're so many Mexicans, that each one can choose different causes. Because in reality all of them are important.

I have two friends who went to volunteer in Africa. The situation they saw in Ethiopia was so striking that they decided they couldn't keep their arms crossed. They opened an organization, that is now called *Cero Pobreza*. Their goal was to raise funds to be able to build a medical attention clinic for that people from the community they visited. Because being over there they realized the closest one was hours away. And that they had no way of getting there.

I loved seeing many friends and people I know join their cause. But still up to this date I haven't stopped listening comments that are more like criticism. One of the things that makes me mad is that they criticize people who are trying to do something for the cause they believe the most in. And it gets me even more angry when the people criticizing, or saying someone should be doing something else, aren't even doing it themselves.

"They should be doing something for their country", some say, about my friends from Cero Pobreza. "They don't have to go that far. There's a lot of poverty in the borders of the city. They should do something here", others say. "And what are you doing?", goes through my mind. Sometimes I don't say it out loud because I know the answer they will give me. Nothing.

The good thing about living in community is the great diversity there is. If you don't share a cause, there's no problem. Everyone has their own. Dedicate yourself to the one you are most passionate about. But without destroying others. Mexico, and the whole world, have millions of problems to solve. And the last thing the world needs is someone who tries to discourage those who believe in something and are trying.

And it's true that no one can do it alone against a problem. But a problem isn't going to get solved without anyone trying to solve it. Take those words into account. They are from a speech Oprah gave to the USC Annenberg graduates:

> *"Americans out of poverty, but who will you be if you don't care enough to try. And what mountains could we move I think, what gridlock could we eradicate if we were to join forces and work together in service of something greater than ourselves? You know my deepest satisfaction and my biggest rewards have come from exactly that. Pick a problem, any problem and do something about it*

because to somebody who's hurting,
something is everything".

I couldn't leave the scholarship program's history that David Noel promoted in his years as a rector.

Do you remember I told you he lived in San Juan de Los Lagos as a young man? It was from there that he went away with only 150 pesos in that bus, to Monterrey, to get his scholarship one way or another. He hasn't forgotten where he comes from after all his success. Not a long time ago I read there has been more than 400 scholarships for students from San Juan de Los Lagos.

It's no coincidence. I'm sure he had a lot to do with that. Thanks David, for being an example, one of those we so lack in Mexico, about insistence, persistence, and coherence.

Let's start reflecting on all the privileges we have. Think about how someone who didn't have them, could have them. This is a good time to start paying our social mortgage. It always is.

Have you ever wondered how your life would be if you would have grown up in totally different circumstances that the ones you have had? What would you be doing right now if your economical future was already ensured?

What if you would have been born in one of the most influential families in the country? Or if you were Steve Job's or Elon Musk's son? Or what would have happened if you would have lost everything when you were a kid?

When I make those questions to myself I remember my grandfather Mario.

He became an orphan at seven. At that short age he didn't have a family to take care of him or one that, at least, gave him affection. Nor people who supported him economically. Even less people who cheered him up or people who believed in him.

How do you carry on when it seems the world is against you?

I don't always tell him, but he's one of the people I admire most in the world. And I'm one of the few lucky ones among my friends who still have their grandparents.

I remember the first semesters of college, when I started Voz *Joven*, my student group. The university opened a leadership workshop for all the groups in campus. Even though it was a Saturday morning, I loved being there, spending my time on what I liked the most. One of many activities, was to take 30 minutes alone, to write on a paper, the name of someone you admired the most. I wrote my grandpa's. Under their name you had to write a letter saying why you admired them. I thought it was like many other activities I had done in other workshops. So, I wrote it thinking no one was going to ever read it.

After a while, when we were all done, they told us what the next step was. We had to call that person and read the letter out loud. I grabbed my phone. I called. He answered. And I started reading what I wrote. I think I didn't even get past the first line when I was already crying.

To be honest, I don't know how he did it. I don't know how someone who has lost the little they had at seven, and who was left without a family, without money and practically nothing, has now everything. But there was a long way in between having nothing and having everything.

To find food, my grandpa had to do several things. Things no one likes to do. Like chase hens and wait for them to lay eggs. When one finally laid one, after several hours, it was now time to open it and eat it raw. Then, with no home to get at the end of the day, garbage dumps were always a choice. There he found tortillas and bread. But when do we throw food away? When it's already rotten and we don't want it anymore. He got excited just by finding it. And he was grateful someone threw it out no matter how it was or looked.

They bullied him at school for the clothes he used. It wasn't new and it wasn't his size. It was the one he could find. Nothing happened if it wasn't his size. He just had to roll up the sleeves. And it was done. They also bullied him for his shoes. Those days he was lucky enough to wear them.

In middle and secondary school there was no one else who gave me better advice than him. They bullied him at school. Just like me. But the difference was that I had someone with experience to teach me how not to take seriously what other people would say to me.

Sometimes I wished the whole world knew his story. Maybe there's someone who needs it. I can imagine many people in Mexico in similar situations to the ones he lived. And the reason why I want people to hear this story is so they know and are sure that you can make it. You have to believe in yourself. Ask for help. Set goals. Between the adversity, deep down inside, find the strength to believe in something better. And do what's in your hands to succeed.

In one of his first jobs, the ones you can aspire to

without a degree, he saw the company's owner over there. "I want to be like that", he thought. And he clung to that idea with all his heart. You need all the persistence in the world to reach your dreams. Mostly, when all the roads life has taken you by seem to go in a worse direction.

Against any forecast, he made it.

Without seeing or learning by himself how it was to live in family, he made one. I don't know if thirty or forty years ago he would have even imagined that those days of chasing hens or looking for food in the garbage were going to end, and that today, after all the suffering he went through, he would be one of the most admired people by his four kids and his fifteen grandchildren. And that he would see his own family grow. That he was going to have a supporting wife in any circumstance. That his kids and grandchildren would grow, study, and have the certainty and assurance of having a supporting family.

My grandpa had a lot of options. Like they say, we can't control everything. But we can control how we react to whatever happens. And he could be mad at this moment about everything he had to live. He could be holding remorse towards those who closed him the doors. He could be a bitter person. He could support no one because no one supported him. And I admire him even more for that. Because he's one of the kindest people I know. Those who always help everyone. The kind of people you could say are helping more than they should. To his family, employees or any stranger.

Every time he can, he donates to a cause. He's always going to have a smile. And if you were in a room full of people with him there, he would be the kindest and most polite person in the room.

He's thankful for what life gave him. He's also aware of how much it costed. But he knows he has to pay his social mortgage. And give back what life gave him. So, someone else can have what he had. And much more.

MAKE THINGS HAPPEN

"Think left and think right and think low and think high. Oh, the thinks you can think up if only you try!"

–

Dr. Seuss

Ideas On Hold

Now what?

The hard work in the government was over. The campaign was too. How weird it felt not to be looking at every news or event I had, or fining places to finish my long checklist.

For almost four years, what I did every morning, was checking the mayor's schedule. I organized my time based on that. Now when I checked it, it was already blank. How was I going to define my own days now?

I looked at the enrollment dates in my university. I had only one semester left to graduate. Finally, after the extra time that took me for switching majors, I was about to finish my years as a college student forever.

The questions I asked myself about what I wanted to do in the future became real and serious. Now, I had to make Plan B. And that plan, had to consider that I would be graduating in six months and would have 100% of my time to my disposition.

I tried to forget about politics and news. The country had already decided what it wanted. I had tried to change things at a national and local level. We lost. I wasn't spending my days like I thought I would. But I felt happy. And for the first time in a long time, I felt totally free and calm.

I didn't want to rush into making decisions to make my new plan, but neither to the so long.

Other times, I had been involved in so many things at once, and always had to quit some of them when I realized I couldn't do everything. And then I thought about more things, I was filled up again with projects and the same thing happened. I didn't want that to be an option this time, or ever. I decided I was going to be focused on a few things for the last six months in college, although I didn't know what they were. Every time a new idea or project showed up, I was going to have to say no, whatever it took.

And I set myself to make my own schedule on my own terms, expectations, and times.

Before getting to class I opened a file I have on my phone and computer notes called "Quotes to remember". It had been a long time since I opened and read it. I write quotes and ideas that I find on books, Twitter, or anywhere which inspire me. Some give me energy. Some make me reflect. And the best ones, motivate me. Every time I open those notes, there's always a quote that gets my attention the most. I think it depends on my mood. This time, the one that I connected with, taking the situation into account, was this:

> *"Do twice of what you're passionate about".*

I have always felt guilty because what i like is very varied and different, that I have only been able to focus on one thing a few times.

Now I had to choose, besides classes, the project that would give me the most energy. Because being honest, I couldn't just be a full-time student. Although I look like a calm person on the outside, I have a lot of energy inside.

And let's not fool anyone. I like and love to think about

the country we can have. It's not just something I can forget after being examples of countries that were in a worse situation than us and now are far better.

After years of working to improve a city, and a campaign where I kept thinking about what we could do to improve the country, besides the things that had happened to me while I was in college, I felt I had many things in my head that I could tell. So, the project I chose to do while I was in my last months at college was to write this book.

And already knew where to start. I still have with me the journal I used in Poland to write some ideas. But I was afraid of starting and not finishing. Because, even though I've had those notes to know where to start, I didn't know how to make it an entire book.

I wanted to write a book since secondary school. When I felt I had found the perfect idea, I started writing and developing the story. Then after some weeks, I realized it was the worst idea in the world, and I quit the project. Months after, i came up with another idea, I would write some pages about that new story, and the same thing happened: I quit when I realized it was a terrible idea. In total, more than ten years like that went by. Because before I believed that if you have an idea, it has to be perfect from the start. And if it isn't, it's not worth working on it.

It had been a long time since the last try. And if I could be creative with clients' projects in my innovation agency, it was time to start being creative for my own personal project.

Now that I had more time to reflect without running from one place to the other, I asked myself "Where do ideas come from?". It's something they ask me a lot because they see I'm involved in different creative projects where I had to develop big strategies or campaigns.

Knowing the answer to that question is important. I'm sure that, to change Mexico and to change the world, anyone is going to need the best ideas to do it. It can also help anyone who wants to change something about their life and find their true purpose for being in this world.

In the classes I had, I heard many people say they aren't creative. And I don't agree. The problem is that creativity is linked to someone's artistic side: use colored pens, make amazing drawings, make a minimalistic design in the computer or invent a song lyric.

When I give consultancy on this topic, there's a comment the clients always make when we're thinking about a solution: "Let's see what you come up with. You're the creative ones". All because of that confusion there is between being artistic and being creative.

I don't agree with those comments. We are all creative. Being human is being creative.

The problem is that we don't practice it during our years in school. And not doing it at that time, makes us not do it when we grow up.

And we don't ty.

You don't have to know how to draw or know how to choose the perfect color combination to say you are creative. You can start asking yourself about how can you do something different, anything. Taylor Harding, from Carolina University, wrote an article for the Arts Education Policy Review, in which he highlights that being creative means much more than imagining or creating something that doesn't exist, like many think. And he proposes a new meaning for the word creativity:

> *"It's that force within each one of us*
> *that appears when we start feeling the*
> *need to answer a question without answer,*
> *or with a bad answer, and we start*
> *imagining more than one new solution".*

I loved it. That simple is to be creative. As simple as making those questions and using your potential to imagine better ways of doing things, even though it's by making little changes. And the possibilities of what someone can discover imagining those answers or changes are unlimited.

But sometimes I feel that imagining and dreaming, is not as common as we think.

I'll never forget the smell of popcorn there was when I walked down the carpeted floors in Blockbuster. I could spend hours choosing a movie to rent (and months could go by to return it after the fines for not bringing it back on time). It's now more comfortable to open your computer and spend those same hours choosing which movie to watch on Netflix.

But remembering the retro will never go out of style.

At the beginning of 2002, Blockbuster launch the presale for "Harry Potter and the Philosopher's Stone". In my house, I spent several days persuading my parents to give me money to register and pay for it. I had to have it. When they saw I really wanted it, they gave me the money and they even took me to confirm the order.

Poor of the employees who answered the phone. I was making two or three daily calls to make sure I knew the date the movie was going to arrive. I was dying to pick it up. And when it finally arrived, we went to Blockbuster, and they asked us which version we wanted. My dad wanted me to ask for the DVD version. We already had a DVD player plugged into the TV. But I only knew the VHS cassettes. So, I clung to the old thing. I still have that cassette along with my other childhood movies. It's a whole collection: The Aristocats, The Lion King, Toy Story, and some of the favorite ones.

Like any little boy, I saw my Harry Potter movie every time I could. But until I went to a cousin's house and I saw her DVD version came with two CDs, I realized I had made a bad choice. In one cd, came the Harry Potter movie. And in the other, there were games and hours of extra material like behind the scenes recordings. It showed the actors, the director, interviews with the book's author, the explanation on how they created special effects and how the arranged the music for every scene. I loved it. But because I was stubborn I had he cassette and wasn't able to change the language, couldn't add subtitles and I had to use a device to rewind the tape every time the movie was over. After that I started buying or renting movies in DVD. Lesson learned.

It could be the weekend and I was at midnight watching behind the scenes from the movies I liked. Since then I enjoy to watch how things are done. I work like this: if I like a book or a movie, I look for interviews or speeches from the writer or the creator where they talk about how they did it (someone else does that?). I always come up with questions about the people I admire the most or my role models, like what time of the day did Obama read in the White House, or where does J.K. Rowling write and how she takes her coffee, where does Dan Brown find ideas and how he researches the details from his stories, or what is Hillary Clinton's method to write speeches, and how does Mark Zuckerberg lead the meeting to evaluate which projects to develop. And I love to look for even the most insignificant details, like which pens they use, what journals they write in, and what their favorite drinks are. I could spend hours searching for videos and watching documentaries about that.

This things creators do, I call them rituals. We all have one. For example, putting on your headphones and listening to your favorite playlist, write on that journal you love, go to the coffee shop where you always find inspiration, prepare a cup of coffee before you work, using your favorite hoodie to do homework, sitting on the same place as always to concentrate, or any other small detail that makes you feel comfortable and makes you have energy to do your activities.

Now that I think about it, looking for those details or watching their interviews is because deep down, I have hope that one of them reveals, in those behind the scenes and interviews, the secret to have such brilliant, extraordinary, innovate and ideas like theirs. But in none of the videos I have seen, and I have seen a lot, has some o the, revealed that secret. Because such secret doesn't exist. Instead, what they reflect is simplicity in everything they do. Their days are like ours.

So then how do they create such incredible things that change the world?

There's a way. I'm an international business graduate. But I also focus on creativity and innovation. Knowing those things has helped me along the way. A lot. Actually, changing Mexico will need very good intentions, that's basic, wanting to do good. But to revolutionize everything, it will take great ideas and actions. Everything starts here.

If someone asks me where good ideas come from, my answer is the one that has worked for me: they come from you. And your capacity for observing and putting attention to what you're living. But exactly that what's most difficult every time.

Does the name Walt Disney ring a bell? I bet it does. He has some experience we can learn from. After creating one of the biggest companies in the history of entertainment, he said this:

"Ideas are the result of curiosity".

And the most famous creative leader in the tech industry, Steve Jobs, said the same, but with different words:

"New ideas come from observing something, talking to people, experimenting, making questions, and getting out of the office".

Both have this in common: the quality of your ideas depends on your capacity to be present in the moment, how much you observe, and get curious about what you see.

I have seen it in the behind the scenes and interviews of

people I admire. They are so passionate about what they do that they spend entire days on that and pay attention to the smallest details. And they keep focused. I don't think, at all, that Mark Zuckerberg spends all day looking at Facebook or Instagram. He even wears the same t-shirt and jeans every day because he doesn't want to spend not even a little bit of his energy deciding which clothes to wear in the morning. Because even that, according to him, can affect attention and concentration he puts into having new ideas.

It has happened to me that I'm driving, but instead of paying attention to the road, I'm thinking about the things I have to finish. And then when I get somewhere, sometimes I even get scared because I realize I don't know how I got there.

How I'm supposed to find new ideas if most of the time I'm worrying about things I have to do? And when I'm doing them, I also can't concentrate because I'm thinking about other things I also have to do later.

Being actually present, paying attention to the moment, isn't something that is promoted a lot in our lives. I have seen signs at some coffee shops asking their customers to turn off their phones and enjoy the conversation. Even though those pictures with the signs go viral on Facebook, who does what they say? It's more normal (and sadder) that you're with someone and while you talk about something, that someone is looking over their phone and even texting.

This last semester, they opened a space in my university to practice mindfulness, which is basically meditating and trying to forget about everything for a while. Steve Jobs never stopped doing it. He even called it a discipline. This is in his biography, written by Walter Isaacson:

> *"If you just sit and observe, you will see how restless your mind is. If you try to calm it, it only makes it worse, but over time it does calm, and when it does, there's room to hear more subtle things - that's when your intuition starts to blossom and you start to see things more clearly and be in the present more. Your mind just slows down, and you see a tremendous expanse in the moment. You see so much more than you could see before".*

If he said it, it must be true. And for those who need some more evidence about the power of meditation, there are studies that show doing mindfulness boosts your creativity because it stimulates your brain in different ways and makes you pay more attention, what makes you more open to new ideas. And it also activates your divergent thinking.

An experiment showed that people who don't meditate had more cognitive stiffness compared to those who meditate regularly or every now and then. In the same experiment, those who don't meditate tended to solve problems with old ideas. Who wants old ideas?

So, no, meditating is not something just for hippies. It's for everyone who wants to know themselves, explore even the deepest place in them and find peace for their daily activities.

In some companies they are even promoting meditation for their employees, because it's been proved that doing it also improves the work environment.

That's why I got into yoga. I wanted to relax and at the same time improve my own capacity to concentrate and being more present in, in the present. That has helped me observe and listen more and, as a result, it has helped me have better ideas.

Next time you have a problem to solve, or you're sitting with a journal looking for new ideas, take ten minutes, sit with your legs crossed, start to breathe slowly and deeply.

Don't try to stop your thought. But observe, or better said, feel, how many they are and about what. Try to think slower, but at the same time, try to pay more attention to each one of them. Start feeling your own body after that. Pay attention to the small noises you hear. Keep breathing deeply. You will find a part of you that you hadn't found before.

There are YouTube videos that help you have a good meditation if you're a beginner. I still use them sometimes.

After a lot of time being stressed, doing yoga and meditating wasn't the only thing I had to do to calm myself. If I read before, after we lost the election I started to read even more. Now I'm at a point where not reading daily is not an option. Books help me relax and make me disconnect from my tasks. And the best of it all: they give me ideas. When it's still daytime and I turn off my Kindle after reading for a while, I feel full of energy to do everything I thought about while reading. If it's nighttime and I'm sleepy, after reading, I reflect until I fall asleep. But starting or ending the day reading a book is very different to when I'm on Twitter or watching Instagram stories. The first thing calms me, opens my mind, and makes me have more ideas, and the latter makes me get FOMO and feel unproductive.

I say choosing a book is like choosing the person you're going to have a conversation with, for hours and entire days. Just like choosing your friends, there are book that are like discussions about facts or events. There are books where you discuss about people. And books where you discuss ideas, actions, and projects. What I do is find a balance. I almost always read a non-fiction book, like business, politics, or innovation, like the one I read about Michelle Obama's life, and at the same time I read some fiction, like Dan Brown's thrillers or James Patterson's which intrigue me and make me flip the pages (electronic ones) as fast as possible.

Some years ago, I opened my Goodreads profile to have a count of the books I've read. Something happens with that app. I have always had it. But I can never keep it up to date. What does work really well for me is the list of pending books to read, because it connects with your Amazon purchases. That way I avoid double searches. And they send me emails with reminders. They are like notices that tell you "stop buying more books and go read these that are awaiting you".

Until 2018 I read "Create or Die", by my second favorite

journalist, Andrés Oppenheimer (the first one will always be Denise Dresser, I'm sorry Andrés). He published it in 2014. I don't know what happened to my pending book list that this one staid at the bottom of the list for four years (thanks, Goodreads). It's better to say this late than never: I do recommend it. It has stories and interviews with amazing people who are transforming and revolutionizing the world.

In the chapter where he talks about education, there's an interview with Salman Khan, the founder of Khan Academy which is to learn any subject from school online. First, he explains how the educational model that is still used in the world's schools and universities, is the one the king of Prussia established in the 18th century, just like it keeps being today: with the purpose of creating a working class, obedient and respectful of the authority.

When I read that, I sat down on my bed instantly. I got excited because something like that had been in my head those days:

*"The new economic realities don't need
an obedient and disciplined working class
anymore, that only has basic reading,
math, and social knowledge. Today's*

world needs a working class of creative
and curious people that keeps getting
educated during their whole life".

Khan said it, and many more, like academics and experts on the matter. But the educational model is still the same than four hundred years ago. It seems like a joke.

Many times, I asked myself what was I doing in a classroom listening a professor talk telling me exactly what was being him on his slides. It was easier for him to send us an email with the file and we could read it at home or at a coffee shop. Or even easier: look up the class online, in YouTube, or an academic online site like Coursera or Udemy. But there I was, doing something unnecessary and old fashioned.

Not all my teachers were like that.

My generation was touched by classes like International Perspective. The professor Elizabeth, or Ely, handed us a lecture calendar from the beginning. It was strictly mandatory to read before getting into the classroom. If you didn't do it, everyone would know, because there was a discussion before class started. You had to be well prepared with your arguments. She didn't go there with us to read slides. She went there to make us think, analyze and debate.

Another class, in the last semester, was about solving a business case every week. Those cases were published by Harvard Business Review. You had to read at home, and then we discussed the problem in class, and in the end, you had to prepare your analysis and solution in your team.

Those were my favorites, the classes where they taught us to think. But from more than fifty classes, very few were like that. And after spending my whole life studying, I can ask myself this question: where, from middle school to college, was something that promote creativity, new ideas and problem solving? Nowhere.

It seems that everything is fine, until you want to sit to think creatively. Until you're in the middle of some situation and you need to find a solution. Or until you're looking what to do to fix Mexico's problems. There's where we struggle to find the best ideas and where we realize we lack creativity.

There's a drawing online of kids forming a line and entering for the first time to the classroom. Above every kid there's their own imagination cloud, like ideas are normally represented on drawings. But the teacher, at the entrance, starts cutting those clouds with scissors and gives them all a squared shape as they are going in. The message is clear. The education system we have not only stops creativity. It also tries to make us all think the same way.

In Mexico and the world, we're going to have more inventors and creators, in any topic, creatives and scientific, social and corporate, if these two things happen: if there's a link between companies, research centers and universities, like Salvador Alva proposes, and when in schools, from kindergarten to graduate, level they stop teaching us to be squared and all the same. Maybe in that time it worked, because it was the industrial revolution and they needed technical and repetitive jobs. But clearly at this time that educational system doesn't work anymore.

There's a pyramid that tries to show how can humans learn. On the top, there's listening, with only 5% of retention. Then there's reading with 10%. After that comes watching and listening audiovisual material with 20%, and making a demonstration with 30% of retention. We call all these passive learning methods. Then we have the ones I like. The co-operative methods. Taking part on a group discussion, with 50% retention. Practice or do something, with 70%. And do and teach others, 90%. It's summed up on the Chinese proverb that goes:

"What I hear I forget. What I see, I remember. What I do, I understand it".

Since I knew that, I always try to tell someone the things I read or learned the day before. That way I don't forget. With this pyramid I could also understand why I liked more the classes where they made me think, discuss on groups, or solve problems and chaos. Because I learned the best that way.

That's where education needs to go. Where there are always situations for students to find solutions. Every classroom has to be the best environment to be creative and to learn how to develop leadership. It's what the world needs more of.

My parents say that when I was 4 or 5, I woke them up, literally every day, so they would play Toy Story for me. I'm officially a Pixar fan. Since the 90s. And still, now at 25, every time I see one of their films I still wonder how they can create masterpieces again and again. To start, how do they come up with those ideas for those creative and different stories (that make us all cry)? Monsters that scare to have electricity or that go to the university. A house with balloons that floats in the air with an old man and a boy. A clown fish that can't find his son in the ocean. Toys worried about being replaced by new ones. And then we have Miguelito looking for his ancestors in the Land of the Dead. They're creative geniuses!

They went through many difficult situations before their productions were successful. Like in the best stories, theirs is full of failures. Even financially speaking, Pixar went almost bankrupt. The only thing that had left was that Edwin Catmull, the founder, and his team, wanted to make their dream come true, one they had in the 60s: make an animated film by computer. The company was sold. Then rescued. Up for sale several more times. And they weren't even making films. To get money, they made some special effects and produced TV ads for a gum company. Very different to what they are now: creative leaders and a role model. They are already part of Disney and a global role model for good ideas.

I don't just admire their creativity. If you think about it, every movie they do is in a completely different world. But that doesn't matter. They always make us connect with emotions, feelings, and situations characters go through until we feel part of it. Like when everybody was crying in the very first minutes of Up.

Since I found out a few years ago that they were

producing a movie about *Día de los Muertos*, I knew it was going to be amazing. And it was. I remember that by the end more than half of the people who went to see Coco were crying.

Even though it's a Mexican movie, it does show very well a lot of our values and traditions.

And who doesn't like to watch the show on the Oscars 2018 with Gael García Bernal singing? While Guillermo del Toro was winning his Oscar for Best Director.

After those Oscars, The Times published an article titled: "How Mexicans took Hollywood". The British journalist remembers how President Trump, once tried to define Mexicans as drug dealers, criminals, and rapists. In his article, he replies:

> *"Could I suggest an alternative?*
> *Visionaries, role models, and Oscar*
> *winners. It has a nice touch".*

That reply is perfect for tweeting it and going viral.

I thought the process to make incredible productions that have won the most important awards in the film industry could be something like: the director comes up with the best idea. He calls the scriptwriter and they write the story. It has to be finished in a few months. They present the project to the company's directors. They approve it. They work on the animated scenes. They record the voices. They add the music. And done. The movie gets to movie theaters and everyone talks about it. It's a success and all the news talk about the money they're making, critics give them the best review, and experts nominate it to the awards they will surely win.

That's the creativity stereotype I talked before. Thinking that you have to get it all perfect since the beginning. And it's weird because no one tell us it should be like that. We think that all the geniuses came up with their brilliant ideas just like that. Simply because they were creative.

In my job and in my life, I had moments like this: it could be midnight and I was still in front of my computer. With a blank page, when after many hours, I should already have a message, a finished script, a task or project ready to send. But I wrote something and erased it. I closed my computer. And I left to do something else. Instead of just doing it, I was waiting for the perfect moment to feel inspired. I always thought that it had to be when your body, mind, and soul felt ready.

This is true: inspiration is overrated. We give it more

power than we should. I didn't realize it until I read "Creativity Inc." by Pixar's director, Edwin Catmull. What I learned: they don't leave it all to inspiration. They see creativity like a process. A very long and frustrating one. These are words from Pixar's director:

> *"A lot of us have a romantic idea about creativity: a solitary visionary has an idea all of a sudden about a movie or a product. Then the visionary leads a team and overcomes everything until they make that promise a reality. Truth is that's not my experience at all. I have met many people that I consider creative geniuses, not just in Pixar or Disney, and I can't remember anyone who has been able to express clearly at the beginning when the adventure started. According to my experience creative people find their invention through time and a long and never-ending fight".*

Take this example. Monsters Inc. The original idea of the movie was about a 40-year-old man who starts seeing monsters who go everywhere with him. That story is totally different from the one about Sully, Mike Wazowski and Boo. They spent months developing the story with the first idea, making sketches, writing dialogues. Recording voices and animating. And every time the team in charge presented the work to the company's team, they started changing little details about the story. Imagine how many things they had to change so the result was the movie we all know!

That's how they do it. They have a very imperfect idea. And they get into what they call an *"iterative process"*. Going back to something you already worked on. Thinking about it again. Creativity is a re-work. They say it's 5% inspiration and 95% frustration. That's why it's important that you love what you do. Because whatever it is, if you want it to be great, it's going to take a lot of re-work. If they spend two, three or four years perfecting a story, you can also do the same with your projects and ideas. But don't leave them because you think they're not good.

Another example. Facebook started being a website only Harvard students could see. It had only one section with pictures of two students, and you clicked the one you liked the most. That was it. I bet no one imagined back then that ten years later Facebook would have more users than an entire country's population. And that we would use it to get in touch with people from all over the world and see the breaking news (and that it was even going to affect people's votes on the presidential election).

And just like those stories, there are thousands. So never feel guilty, sad or frustrated for not having a good idea. Just take a blue pen, choose a journal, breathe, look what's around you, note down your ideas, and work on them. Make that idea be good. Forget about being inspired. Just do it. The next day, check your old notes. I'm sure you'll come up with something to improve it. Take more notes. That way you'll be doing what they do in the world's most creative company. And in many others that have changed the world.

They sell a mug with this quote on Amazon:

"Let your actions do the thinking".

The author is Charlotte Brontë, the sister of Pride and Prejudice's writer.

We should all drink coffee from that mug. Maybe remembering it daily we can have more ideas and improve them while we do them. Just the way many successful people and companies did it.

"The best way of starting something is to stop taking about it and start doing it"

–

Walt Disney

What Matters

Before, people though their ideas were the most valuable thing on Earth. Be it an invention, a business, a story, a product, they were terrified about someone hearing their idea. When they talked to a friend about it, it was like in a spy movie. Imagine a guy with a coat and hat so no one recognizes him. He meets someone at the entrance of a bar or cafe with few people inside.

They make sure no one is following them and they sit far away in the dark. The one with the idea takes off his hat, and before he risks to talk about it, he then looks everywhere to verify no one is listening.

We're more than 7 billion people in the world. We're full of ideas. And the more you share them and get people involved, the better. It's important to be creative. Improve every time. But this chapter is about what's next. And what really matters.

In the end, the value of an idea depends on the use you give to it. Thomas Edison said it.

It's happened to me more than fifteen or thirty times that someone launches a new app or product or they start a new business and I think: "Ah! I thought about doing that!". And I'm sure it's happened to you too. The famous "I thought about it before". Steve Jobs said at an interview on the 90s: "taking credit of ideas is the easiest thing". The hardest is to make them happen.

Something like that happened when I tried to launch my foundation. It stayed as an idea. Even though I was planning it for a year. To start, I took three months to choose the name. Then, I took even more to choose one cause.

But it stayed like that. Just an idea.

So, this century isn't about ideas, like the last one. This one is about execution. If you look anywhere, you'll see that. Who's making progress? Those who are executing their plans. Those who are making their ideas happen.

Those who instead of thinking, do things and improve them.

It's not easing. Executing and not just dreaming has become harder and harder. Distractions are everywhere. Excuses are too. And fears.

You can do the math yourself. The day has 24 hours. You spend almost eight hours sleeping (I hope). Then you're left with only sixteen. If you take an hour to have breakfast, lunch and dinner, you have thirteen hours left. What are you doing with them?

A study by the Internet Mx Association about the time Mexicans spend online, found out that on average we spend 2 hours and a half on social media. Almost three hours. Some days it can be more (thanks Netflix). Ok. Then from the thirteen hours, only ten are left. We still have to count the time you take to shower, get dressed, and get ready. And the time you take to get anywhere. The talks with people and friends. The calls. Everything that happens in a normal day.

Loosing time is like *ant spending* in finance. You can buy coffee and snacks daily thinking that it's only fifty or a hundred pesos. But when you ad it at the end of the month, it was 3000% more than you expected.

The most recent version of iOS has a screen time count. And a notification count. A week after I installed it, I got scared by the numbers. First, the number of hours I spend on my phone was the same Internet Mx got in the study. Three hours daily. Without counting the time on my computer. It also counts when you check your phone for anything. Eighty-five times a day, on average. Notifications scared me the most. Apple counted 160 notifications daily on average.

If someone asked me how much time I spent on my phone before I saw that, I would've said almost nothing. I was one of those who felt proud of not being on their phone like everyone else. Besides, since we lost the election, I got into yoga and started organizing my schedule, so I thought I didn't need my phone as much as that time when I had to check it all day long. But numbers are numbers. And they mean a lot.

It starts there. Asking what are you doing with your time. Because it's not relative. Like many of the things we need in real life, time management isn't something we learn at school. Making your ideas happen completely depends on the time you spend on them. And you're not going to achieve anything if you don't spend any time on that.

When I talk to people about plans or projects they have and I ask them when they will do it, I always hear: "next year", "I have to plan it first", "I'm really busy now". Then I realize it's still an idea, not a plan. Not an action. The day someone shows me a calendar divided in stages, and that they're following it, I don't know how I will react. Maybe I'll get excited and hug them. And I'll admire them more.

Making your idea doesn't have to be from one day to the other. Good things take time. That's why it has to be something you're passionate about and that gives you energy. Because it needs a lot of your time. And your best effort.

Eleanor Roosevelt, the first lady of the US to be an activist at the same time, once said:

> *"The future belongs to those who believe*
> *in the beauty of their dreams".*

It's always going to be true. Because once you start making ideas into plans and actions, you'll need it a lot. Many nights without sleep. A lot of time. Frustration while you re-work your idea. Testing and mistakes.

And you can even get a huge number of critics, like

anyone else who's believing in their dreams.

If she wasn't full of energy and passionate about thinking of solutions to solve social problems from that time, like ending inequality, maybe the Universal Declaration of Human Rights wouldn't have been signed in the UN. And even though we admire her now, back in her day she was criticized by being "too active and independent" for her time. They told her over and over again that it didn't fit her first lady role. But she sticked to her values, her plan, and she didn't keep dreaming about what she could do. Instead, she did it.

Remembering, sometimes, her dedication and career, and those of the people who I admire, makes me think about what I'm passionate about and not. And to be active. None of them got to the point where they do nothing anymore.

I know that taking the first steps is sometimes the hardest. But who defines how hard or easy something's going to be? You do. And how much you want to wish something.

Everyone lives with their style. But a study found that those who don't act on their ideas are too busy, they have a demanding job that absorbs them, and they don't take time to think about their own priorities. Realizing that is the first step.

I have also felt with no exit and drowned in tasks. When I'm like that, I see my calendar and I see the nearest free day. It's like auto torture. Checking the days for a moment of peace. And they're also lessons. It's learning and testing what you like and what you don't. You have to keep filling your days with the first, and getting rid off the latter.

Derek Sivers is an entrepreneur who defines himself as someone who wants to do many things. On his website, he wrote: "I want to make articles, books, websites, music, companies, systems, apps, and especially new ideas". Basically everything. He already sold two of his companies and he's on vacation in Singapore taking advantage of it to keep creating.

I like his focus. In one of his works he also explains what has defined his life: saying no to most things, to put the most time into what he has to do.

When I share something on twitter it's because I want other people to see it too. I also use it for saving thing I like and that I want to remember later. I retweet and like some. Sometimes I find quotes, I copy them, I paste them, and I post them. Like Derek's quote.

"If you're not saying hell yeah! about
something, then say no".

With this in mind, it was easier to do my plan B. My priorities were like this:

- Five classes (the last ones) where I wanted to get the best possible grade.

- Write my book.

- Launch a new food supplement to the market.

That was my short-term plan. My days were divided that way. Instead of planning the swearing-in ceremony for a deputy and making his office the best in the country, I focused on those three things. And on three projects we had in my consultancy agency.

It looks like a lot. But in my plan, I could perfectly make time in a calendar for each of my priorities. I divided them into stages, and I put objectives and deadlines. I told myself not everything had to be perfect. It doesn't happen even in the companies. But I had to follow the plan as best as possible.

Next time I have to make that plan longer. One of the books I also read in that time was the one by Facebook's Executive Director, Sheryl Sandberg. She recommends having a personal plan of eighteen months. In the book she says she has always done it like that. She has her own explanation for that number. She says twelve months would be too short, focused on the short term. And twenty-four months sounds like a lot. Eighteen is perfect.

The worst is when that planning is empty. Not having a plan is not knowing where you're going. Just like it happens to the country and many companies. And this number is like an emergency alert: 99% of people in the world don't plan their personal life. With that, we can understand why many people don't like their job, they are unhappy, or don't find a purpose on what they do.

But it's something we can correct. We just have to adjust and make changes. Like when I switched my major. That day I had to make an Excel with a calendar to know how much time I would take to graduate with the classes I had left.

You can even use a Sunday to make your plan. At least a draft. It doesn't have to be perfect. Actually, the opposite! You'll change it as time goes by. But something will be consistent: you'll be getting to something that you see purpose in. That's a great competitive advantage already.

Besides that, due dates are something that, many studies

and experiments say, works. They are kind of like a pressure for us to achieve the goals we set. It's not the same to say *"I have an idea for an app"* than saying *"I came up with an idea for an app some time ago and I'll launch it on November 10, 2019."* And it's not about exaggerating due dates. Not too late, not too soon. They simply have to be realistic.

Having a calendar has worked a lot for me. I like to set a day and time to the tasks I have. And taking space in my schedule to use it on my projects. Maybe it sounds like too much, but I schedule everything (I don't know why I didn't do it before). Literally everything: even when I go out with my friends, lunch, sometimes even time to read. But again, this is what has worked for me. Each one has to find what works for them.

I know people who are highly effective and use completely different systems than mine. Like checklists on a journal. Some are totally digital like me. Some take a planner everywhere and they note down tasks on an app. Some use Wunderlist and others use Google Tasks. I even know some people who don't keep any control and are extremely capable of remembering everything they have to do. That's not for me. In my world, if it's not written, I know it's not going to happen.

"A written dream with a date, becomes an objective. An objective divided into different steps becomes a plan. And a plan backed up by actions makes your dreams come true", Greg S, Reid wrote, one of the authors and most famous speakers on entrepreneurship. It sounds inspiring. And it's also realistic. To prove it, Gail Matthews PhD, from the Dominican University in California, made an experiment with two groups of people: the ones who wrote their dreams and planned, and those who didn't. She discovered that, like the quotes says, those who write their goals, have 42% more chance of reaching them. Just because they wrote it.

For anyone who's skeptical, this is science. Not just motivational quotes.

On the first days of class they gave us a calendar with the important days for graduation. One made me get in panic. The day of my degree exam, the CENEVAL. It would have questions about each and every class I had. I felt I knew nothing, even though I was already on my last semester and I loved International Business.

In September, a month before the exam, I printed out a four-hundred-page guide to start studying. I was afraid of failing and everyone realizing I didn't know anything and I wasn't good for that career. And the worst: if I failed, I was also going to know I chose again a career that wasn't my thing.

Part of the impostor's syndrome is believing that others are doing things better than you. That's why many people spend a lot of time working on the same thing over and over again, without going to the next thing. The famous "perfectionists". This is very common. It happens to me with the projects of some clients. I check them endlessly and I can't be in peace. It happened to me when I got into college when I thought everyone was smarter than me, and now again, with the exam, that I felt I didn't know anything.

If they are exams or school work, there always comes the due date. And it's done. But when it's about personal goals, many people, when they want to do something in their company, or when they want to start their own business, they can spend hours, days and weeks trying to make something perfect, until they get bored and they leave it because it wasn't perfect. And it ends up being another project that was left undone.

When I did my best to present the best final project in

one of my classes, it happened that someone who had done the minimum effort, while being under the professor's expectations, got the same grade as me. It didn't seem fair after one or two nights without sleep because I was planning and rehearsing. It also happened with a lot of clients when it came to preparing a visual project. I focused on thousands of details and in the end, they didn't even realize.

Done is better than perfect. That's one of my new mantras. And I have to keep repeating it to myself every time I'm about to hand in something and I want to review it again and modify it again. It's a way of doing things faster. More importantly: a way of finishing things.

Perfection can many times be the biggest enemy of progress. It makes you work slower and like I said in the beginning, while trying to make it perfect, you end up giving up on what you started. And when you leave things that you had set unfinished, you stop trusting yourself little by little, and you lose the security that you will do what you say. Anne Lamott wrote this:

"Perfectionism is the voice of the oppressor. It will keep you mad all your life, and it's the main obstacle between you

and a first draft that sucks. I think
perfectionism is based on the obsessive
belief that if you run carefully, taking each
step correctly, you won't have to die. Truth
is you'll die anyway and that many people
who don't even look their feet, will live
much better than you, and will have more
fun while they do it".

She was right.

Let's not get confused. Being mediocre is not an option. A minimal effort culture wouldn't do anything to make us keep going. Not like a country or in our personal or professional lives. Actually, we would be going back. But accepting nothing we do will be perfect, gives us space to feel comfortable with the work we do. And be able to, finally, finish it. You don't need to lose and waste all your energy and time in the process.

In 2007 when Apple launched the first iPhone version, besides it was a huge device compared to today's versions, it didn't even have an app store. I'm completely sure they had thought about it before and they were developing it. But because done is better than perfect, they launched the iPhone as it was. Months later they announced an update that included the App Store. And there are always bugs in their operating systems. That's why we get so many notifications telling us to update our phone. But if they waited for all their products to be perfect to launch them, they would have never announced any of them.

One professor who lived in China while she was teaching and getting her master's degree, realized that every time she made a question in the classroom, there was an absolute silence. Even though they had read everything and they knew the answer, there wasn't even a word. It got to the point where she had to make direct questions pointing at someone or saying someone's name. Not even that ended the problem. Because every time that happened, the one who had to answer, first made a panic face, and then started talking really slowly. After a while she found out that everyone was afraid to make a mistake and being embarrassed. That's something shocking and common in some Asian cultures, like in Korea, where they don't take risks, in any way, to lose their honor.

That's the clearest example of the impostor's syndrome. The students knew the answers because they were prepared, but they didn't think they prepared enough. They wanted to be perfect. And because they felt they weren't, they didn't participate. In Mexico, the professor joked saying that if she was giving the class here, everyone would have wanted to talk without even reading before. At least we trust we can handle things well.

Be careful of not being ever on the place the Chinese students were. We have to take care of what we do and say so both things go with our personality, doing a good job and making a good effort, but without being afraid to make a mistake. If not, we're never going to learn or grow from our mistakes. Because we'll be avoiding them. And we'll get stuck where we are. Without progress.

They are decisions we have to start making.

Some of my projects do need more attention than others on small details and I have to spend more time on them. Some others don't. But when I'm doing something and I realize I'm spending more time than I should, I take a deep breath and I take a look at my progres. Then I realize it's already enough to call it finished work. And that's it. Time to move on.

Many times, I already know what I have to do, but I just can't do it. I can't find the energy, or I don't feel concentrated or prepared to do it. And a vicious circle starts. I stress because I have many things to do, but I don't do them. And I start looking at pictures on Instagram or watching something on Netflix. But I don't enjoy it. I do it stressed. And the closest the deadline is, the more pictures and episodes I see. Until I do it last minute, under pressure, and I realize it wasn't as hard or challenging as I thought. Has that happened to you? It's called procrastination. There are studies that prove that procrastinating, isn't as bad as it seems, like I thought before. But we have to be able to tell the difference. One thing is procrastinating and another thing is being lazy.

In Wisconsin University, Jihae Shin, did an experiment where she asked everyone to present innovative business ideas. She divided people in three groups. To group one, she asked to hand in the task immediately. Group two played a little before doing the same. And grow three was asked to postpone handing the idea. Can you imagine which one was the most creative? The last ones. Shin's conclusion was that one of the benefits of leaving everything to the last minute is that it promotes creativity, because by taking time to do things, your minds thinks of more possibilities and beat around the bush.

Experiments like these have made psychologists around the world not have a conclusion on procrastination and people's productivity. Some have an agreement and classify them in two: active procrastinators and passive ones. The first ones procrastinate a task while they're doing another one. The passive ones, procrastinate, forget, and also don't do anything else. We have to be like the first ones. Don't do everything too early, but also don't forget it or do it days or months after it should have been ready. This is a good quote to remember:

> *"A virtue is a voluntarily acquired disposition, which consists on a middle term between two bad extremes, one for excess and the other one for defect".*

Find middle ground. And look how to procrastinate well, like Johae Shin's first group. If you're going to procrastinate something, do it so it's better. To have more time to think or innovate more. Not to leave it alone.

Writer Paul Graham said that good procrastination is avoiding tasks to do real work. And you decide what real work is. Try to make it what's going to get you closer to your goals. Part of growing is learning to do that. To choose your battles right. Things you're going to spend your attention and effort on. You can't do everything. And not everything's worth it. Time is one of the most valuable things you have.

In my case, the more I like something and find a purpose, less I procrastinate. I've been part of projects I'm so passionate about that I can spend days without realizing, not replying messages, cleaning up my room and not hand in homework. The difference is that one thing will give me better results and others won't.

In the 1800s, philosopher Henry David Thoreau, realized everyone had things to do. He took a time to think. "It's not enough to be busy. Ants are too. The question is, how are you getting busy?", he wrote. Two hundred years later and it has been something important to remember all the time.

For someone who wants to write a book, open an organization, produce a short film, start a business or finish a project, is very common to say "I don't have time, I'm too busy". We have to clean the house, do laundry, feed the dog, go to the bank, finish an essay, go grocery shopping, pick up the kids, answer messages and emails, and also visit the family and go out with friends.

Let's not fall into that illusion that the more tasks we finish, the more we grow. You can spend an entire day working on something that will take you to something bigger and closer to achieving your goals, or you can spend all day finishing ten of fifteen day to day tasks that, even though you think you are being pretty efficient and productive, won't make you get ahead on your plans.

Most of the Sunday nights, I check my week's schedule. I note down the priorities on a journal, and once they are there, I adjust the times. I try to do the most important thing in the morning. My favorite days are the ones where I can split the time and do something in the morning, like having a creative meeting with a potential client, and write in the afternoons. Or the other way around.

Some days I wake up, go to my yoga class, and I have to spend the day doing paperwork, invoices, send emails, wash my car, clean my room, and feed and walk Kira. Even though I know those things won't make me reach my goals, like I said, I have to do them and that's why I scheduled them.

Some months before switching majors, when I was still in Industrial Engineering, I was obsessed with being the most productive and efficient person. Because I had a lot of activities at the time, I organized events and got involved in different organizations and groups, you can imagine my long list of tasks. In my desperation for doing more things and achieve more goals in less time, one they that I couldn't do it anymore, I went to the library in my university to look for a book I saw online: "The 7 habits of highly effective people" by Stephen Covey. I found one of its first editions. I went down to the first floor to get it. I handed my card. I ran to my car. I stopped to get a coffee. I got to my living room. And I started reading.

Nothing made sense to me. Everytime I read the next page I didn't lose hope that I would find the secret. But I never did. In the end I felt like I lost my time reading that instead of being productive.

I know why I didn't find anything to help me be highly effective, like the title said. I didn't realize it at that time, but i read it looking for an approval to my own system for doing things. I wanted to find quotes to be strong, keep focused and keep doing what I had to do. Before I had a radical idea about being efficient. I thought it was being super stressed. I got full of things to do in one day. I tried to solve everything right away. I made calls and got even more tasks. I did the urgent. I slept very little (and I was proud about it). I was always tired. I had a lot of coffee and a lot of junk food. I don't know why I got that stereotype of an efficient person. Maybe it was because of a book or movie. I just thought that's how it worked. And that I had to get used to it.

That's not the way. And it was hard to learn that. There were months where I got stomach problems for two or three weeks. I started to eat healthier, but my body didn't mind it. It was like Madagascar, the movie. Melman was a giraffe who was always sick. And he already knew by heart the medicines he had to take. He didn't think about anything else other than his health. My friends and sisters said I was like Melman. Always with some issue and medicine in my backpack. When someone got sick they knew they had to ask me for advice.

It was only stress. Now I don't get sick. Just once, and it was a cold. It was just one week that I couldn't go to yoga (coincidence?). But I recovered with ginger, lemon, and grapefruit shots.

I always like to look for natural food's properties. Like matcha powder: they're the green tea leaves left to dry under the sun, and then they grind them. It tastes delicious with almond milk and some sweetener. It has ten times more antioxidants than a normal tea. And besides giving you energy, it also helps you relax.

That's how we had the idea to launch our own brand of natural food supplements. My business partner and I were planning this for months. But we hadn't done it. This was like a little experiment to prove that done is better than perfect.

It was August. We were making plans to launch our first food supplement, and we thought the fall or the end of the year would be a good date. There were many things to do. We already had the formula. But we were missing the tags, the permits, the online store, taking pictures for advertisement. Practically everything was missing.

We remembered the quote, and that motivated us to change our plans. Instead of waiting months, we set the launching date on the next Monday.

Did it work? Yes. On Monday, like we planned it, we launched the online store and a campaign. Was everything perfect? No. Actually, the first tags looked a bit blurry. And making the shipments costed three times more than we thought. But it was done. We kept improving over time. Some changes had to be quick, like that shipment price. Some others could take a little longer.

Maybe if we waited months, and we had done everything slowly, the mistakes would have been the same. Who knows?

but if someone doubts if done is better than perfect, I already proved it.

And I also proved the opposite. That endless plans, without organization, without a plan and a strategy, get you nowhere.

After proving done is better than perfect, when I wanted to make the food supplement company we had built in record time official, I remembered some articles and tweets I saw about how easy it was now to open a company in Mexico. It was the moment for finding out if it was true or not.

Before, you needed minimum capital of fifty-thousand pesos and the help from a public notary to create a company under a mercantile society of two people. Many people and organizations changed this, and now there's another option.

It was in 2015 when the Mexican Entrepreneur's Association launched an initiative to reform the law and allow entrepreneurs to open companies digitally and free. It was a whole national movement. Many people signed the petition to make it happen. And in the end, they did it. And they didn't stop there. They keep proposing and looking to take down any obstacle so that we have better opportunities and anyone can open a company.

Doing it was harder than saying it, because the information online was very confusing. In all Google, I only found a guide for my case. It was easier that way.

So I opened the Economy Secretary's website, I chose the process I wanted, and I started. It was true. You don't need fifty-thousand pesos, a partner, or a public notary to make your company. The government made a new regime called Anonymous Simplified Society to support entrepreneurs. So when you register your company, it's something like: Your New Company, S.A.S.

I couldn't believe it. We were on a government website, making the process to create a company. Just like they announced, it was being easier and everything was digital and automatic. The system asked for information and electronic signatures. I felt proud of the Economy Secretary for changing a complicated and long process to a smart system, where you just follow simple steps, where anyone with internet can start a company.

In the end the system gave us a constitutive act. And I was still shocked. A formal company in hours!

I started to read the files, and I realized there were blank spaces that shouldn't be there. And when I wanted to go on with the process, I couldn't even log in.

It was too good to be true. I talked over the phone to report the issue and they told me the process failed and the company wasn't correctly registered on the system. After weeks waiting, they erased the process so we could start over. It took us 6 weeks to complete the process, not hours or days like they promised.

But I'm still optimistic that my case was an exception.

Anyway, this new way of quickly creating new companies should be promoted and be used to avoid informality and the lack of small businesses growing. It's a good solution to make entrepreneurs make their plans happen, dream big, so they can one day have a big company like the best and most valuable ones in the world.

While I was working in my city's government, there was a great opportunity to improve public transport. It wasn't my area, but I really like it. That's why I researched and read all the details. The plan was really good. It was about changing the buses, naming each station, a new cost system depending on the destination, new routes, among other things. I got really excited and I thought I would soon leave my car at home and use public transport. I did it in other countries and I like it. You can walk, take the metro or bus to get anywhere in the city.

There are many reasons, excuses and problems related to budget, the unions and agreements between them. Of course, many people opposed progress. Like the own transport companies. The mayor never made them understand that if they updated themselves, competed and offered a better service, people would prefer them. They would even have more profit.

But in the end, it didn't happen. We still have, like many other cities in Mexico, a really bad public transport system that is better to avoid. This lacked insistence and persistence. Any change needs it. Even fighting against the current. That's why our ancestors have done so we can be here.

How many governments had amazing ideas and even got to the point to make well and structured plans real, to then end up not doing them? I think it's a direct result from choosing representatives and politicians who talk a lot, and very pretty, but do little.

I've said it many times, Mexico has the potential, the good intentions, and the good ideas. Governments, and also each one of us. We're clever, creative, and fun. But we have to get to the other side. That's the only thing we're missing. Start and finish. If we get used to being doers, many things will change in our personal life and our environment.

Whatever you have in mind, don't leave it at an idea. Note it down. Make a plan. Do it. That's what matters. Open your notes and write "better is done than perfect" and get used to being a doer.

I'm one of those who love creativity. That's why the last chapter was about that and how to have good ideas and re-work them. But when you do them, you'll see they are better than you thought. If not, you know what to do. Improve them. Don't leave them. Take the first step. And do whatever you have to do to finish.

Dare to work on big things. Many people don't do it because they're afraid. They think the more things they do, or the bigger their projects are, the more problems they'll face. It completely depends on how you see it and how you react. I see it this way: if problems are big, solutions have to be big too.

Rodrigo Echávez published this quote:

"We all have the same fears, only ones

*use it as impulse, and others, as an
excuse".*

I know about those who use fear to take impulse. Because if you don't believe in yourself and dare enough to work on your own plans, maybe you'll end up working on someone else's.

Keep in mind that great things need time and effort. If it was easy, anyone would do it. But you're not just anyone.

After some years, I'm sure that, if I read Covey's book again now, I would be nodding and getting excited with every word. I can't blame anyone for not understanding it at that time. I was 18. I was just in the process of getting a more open mind.

"We build too many walls and not enough bridges."

–

Isaac Newton

Out of The Box

I couldn't say no to everything that came up after making my plan for the next six months. I learned not to be too harsh or too flexible with my calendar. But it wasn't like before, that I thought of something that seemed amazing and left everything I had to get into that idea. I just said yes to things I knew were worth it, that wouldn't take much time, but that would make me grow as a person and professional.

One of those things I didn't consider was going to a Kybernus workshop. I was invited and said yes instantly. Kybernus is a group that promotes leadership in Mexico with public, private, and social organizations. I heard a lot about them in the news and I saw some of their activities on social media. And that workshop was the first open to the public. Anyone could go.

In that workshop I met an entrepreneur that, from a cowering office in Mexico, sells matcha in Spain with ads through Instagram. She also helps her followers be more productive, eat healthier, and be more focused on their goals. That's the kind of things millennials know how to do. Connect ideas, people and places, and take what we know to help others. We know that not being physically there doesn't mean not being there. We can get to a lot of people thanks to online tools, but we can't only think locally, but also on the impact we can have in the world.

There are lots of people on Instagram and Twitter who can do what they love the most and makes them happy, and also pay all their expenses and have a comfortable lifestyle. In my city, or in real life, I have seen few people like that. The traditional idea of finding a job is still normal. That's why, knowing someone who is following his passion, and who was breaking the traditional idea, excited me and made me thing about the many possibilities there are when you try to find your purpose in life. And also in all the opportunities we don't see. Mostly, the business opportunities. They're bigger than you can think.

Even more in Mexico. We are still a manufacturing country, but that doesn't mean other markets and industries in the country aren't growing.

We're a power. It looks like only foreigners know it. Many international leaders think that Mexico isn't making the most out of his potential. It's like when you don't know what you have until you lose it. If that's the case, this is what we have: the perfect geographic location, great farmer products, natural resources, and perfectly capable people. We're ready to start to create products and offer services. And ready to make the most out of our location to be the central point between Latin America with Europe and Asia.

One of my favorite teachers, Renato Balderrama, expert on Asia, always told us in his classes that we had to open our eyes and take the opportunities we had. He told us he couldn't believe all the things we didn't take. For example, we live in Coahuila, which has one of the best agricultural universities in Latin America right around the corner, and living in a state with the highest indexes on agricultural production, "Why aren't you seeing how to profit on those things and create an innovative product to export it?" You have the knowledge and the farming talent, you are international business students and have time, "What's missing?"

Very simple: We lack action, passion, and ambition.

He told us a story about a Mexican who started exporting. What he did was check the list of products that other countries were asking for. One of the things he found on that list, was jellyfish. Yes, those blue things that can stick to your skin and burn you can be eaten. According to that study, they were only a few in Asia. And Mexico had a lot of them in its beaches. With the team he needed, he began to collect jellyfish in the coasts, applied for an investment fund from the government to find the right way to pack it, keep it fresh, and export it to Japan. Renato told us we should be looking for opportunities like that all the time. Global opportunities.

The time we're living in is one where the world is more connected every time. And even though some nationalist leaders have appeared in some countries, the reality is that no country is self-sufficient, now or ever. Ans this is something we can take advantage of. We all need everyone.

Fortunately, Mexico has open doors thanks to all the treaties with more than 46 countries, and we are part of the World Trade Organization. But it looks like Mexicans only listen to one: the US. The country where we keep exporting 80% of our products.

My degree, International Business, was born at the same time where the presidents of Mexico, the US, and Canada signed NAFTA, in the nineties. We joked in class, some were serious, that if NAFTA wasn't renegotiated and it was cancelled we would be out of the game and our studies wouldn't be worth anything. I was sure that, if it wasn't renegotiated, we would be the most needed professionals by companies. And that there would be thousands of entrepreneurs doing their thing. Because there was going to be no other option than to start exporting more to Europe and Asia in a very visionary way.

In the end, the new deal was sign on the last day of Enrique Peña Nieto's government, after more than a year and a half of negotiations. The three presidents, Enrique, Justin, and Donald, approved the agreement in Argentina. It's now called USMCA. They say it's the most innovative deal in the world. We'll have to see. But we have to make the most out of it. It's to just that treaty, also others we have with more countries.

I posted an Insta Story that I was at an event at the University of Monterrey. My friends started texting me thinking I switched universities all of a sudden, in my last semester. But no. Sergio, who graduated from there, invited me to an event. Two people came from Georgetown University! to talk about two topics: commerce, and international anti corruption. When he invited me I couldn't say no, and I cancelled everything that day to go. Some of the most famous people have studied in Georgetown, like President Bill Clinton, first FBI's director, J. Edgar Hoover, and first lady Jackie Kennedy. It would be interesting to listen to anyone who came to Monterrey all the way from Washington.

We were just on the first floor of the building and I was already excited. Everything was very executive. We had to take an elevator to get to the conference place. There was only one elevator and people were already waiting for it. We came close and heard they were speaking English. The elevator arrived, and even though it was small, we all went in. I knew it instantly. It was the Georgetown experts! But we were so tight in the elevator that we were all trying not to make eye contact.

We got to the conference's floor, I registered as a guest and I sat as close as I could.

When the first one started, I was amazed by her way of

speaking in public. She can connect with you immediately because she talks with a good voice tone, sounds natural, demonstrates she's smart, has charisma, and is humble. I didn't know anything about her, but then I googled "Jennifer Hillman". I found her career with videos about her interviews on CNN, BCC, and C-SPAN. Who did I have in front of me? Someone totally passionate about what she does. The kind of people I always love to meet. And the kind of people who give me energy and hope.

The World Trade Organization has 164 members, that is, almost all the countries in the world. One of its main tasks is to solve conflicts that can happen in negotiations between the many countries. They check tariffs, custom duties, they avoid companies doing dumping or any kind of violation, breaches or confusions with the rules they agreed to follow.

The highest court on international trade for the WTO countries is the Appellate Body. It has seven judges. And its leader, Jennifer, had just finished her term. Any commerce aficionado like me, would die to have her experience. I wrote every word she said.

It was great. Jennifer was my new hero. It was about the way Trump is doing international trade and the law implications. She talked about the many attempts from Trump to detach the US from international leadership groups and multilateral institutions. And how they avoided to have new negotiations to get into new markets or let them in. And the great attention to bilateral deficits and how he's looking for reciprocity. To him, trade is a game of sum zero. One where there can only be a winner and everyone else loses.

I don't buy it. It's not about who takes the biggest piece of the cake. The leadership the twenty-first century needs is one where we look to work together to make the cake bigger so it's enough for everyone. I like to think of negotiations that way.

But not him. That's why he announced went out of the Trans-Pacific Partnership (TPP). But Mexico, ladies and gentlemen, is going to be a part of it. And if it's approved, we'll have more opportunities. Everyone. Because that partnership will open new doors in new countries and are markets.

TPP's history is confusing. It's not what we thought it could be. At the beginning it was a project to make a huge economic block between several countries, creating a potential market of 800 million consumers, and the idea of taking down commerce barriers between these countries. Twelve countries signed to become part of it: Mexico, Japan, Australia, Canada, US, Peru, Chili, Malaysia, Vietnam, New Zealand, Singapore, and Brunei. Can you imagine those countries united commercially? The first version, that was never approved, had chapters and articles about internet access for everyone, the free flow and movement of people, the work conditions had to be standardized, protection for investors, intellectual property, environmental policies, and also for the first time, topics from the twenty-first century, like digital content, e-commerce, and the big problem of corruption we deal with daily.

There will be great benefits for Mexico if it gets approved. To start, our potential market would expand. That means we would have the chance of trading with 372 million consumers. And it would be the first time that we have an agreement with Australia, Malaysia, New Zealand, Brunei, Vietnam, and Singapore. Also, we would improve the agreements we already have with Canada, Chili, Japan, and Peru.

If it's hard to get citizens from a single country to agree, imagine how hard it is when so many countries are negotiating. That's why the TPP has been taking some time.

Some of the countries that already signed hope China will join. We would have access to their potential market of more than one billion people, the biggest in the world. But they haven't shown interest. And even though it's not happening for TPP yet, it is for Mexico. Recently, China's ambassador, Qui Xiaoqi, said they are interested on signing a bilateral trade agreement with Mexico. And he also said what we need to do it: leave the fear.

China came late to globalization. Actually, way later than Mexico. But they came all in. And of course, because they're from Asia, they planned everything perfectly.

They have a huge project: go back to being the world's trade leaders, like their ancestors.

There was the silk road before: the commerce network that China used to make business since the first century BC. It went through all the Asian continent all the way to Europe and Africa. Thinking about it, I think they invented the International Business career without realizing it.

The project of the century, like China's President, Xi

Jinping, called it, is called "One belt. One road". It's the same idea of the road from the old times, but adapted to the twenty-first century, with all that it means, like investing in technology and infrastructure. And that's going to cost just 5 trillion dollars. And stable and strategic diplomatic relationships for the long term with 70 countries. When they finish with this project, China would have re established its silk road with the countries that make 62% of the world's population.

Many think we have to choose between China and the US. A hard choice. The relationship they both isn't good. I liked what ambassador Chi said about that:

> *"China's position is clear. We don't want a war with the US, because both sides lose. In a trade war, no part wins. This situation can be solved with dialogue. However, we aren't afraid of threats or blackmailing. If he wants a trade war, we will be with him until the end".*

When the US announced they were getting out of the TPP negotiations, the remaining countries had great doubts about the importance of the partnership without that country. And if it was worth it or not. This made it take more time until they realized it was worth it. And

TPP-11 was made. The updated version. Mexico already confirmed. Now we just have to wait for other countries to do the same. It needs six members so it can work. We were the first to do it. If it happens, it would bring many benefits for import and export opportunities, the processes between the countries would improve and the wait times would be shorter. Investment flows would work, tariffs would get lower and it would create more employment. It would get us closer to the twelve economies that are part of it and it would improve information and knowledge flow. It would make us a more global and diversified country.

The US leaving the TPP leaves a leadership spot there. So any developing country could tale its place. Like Mexico or New Zealand.

Everything is on the table. Mexico: this will be our century.

When I thought I had everything in order, my university told me I had to do an activity for my social service.

Even though it's supposed to be the best moment for giving back to the community, many people do something where there's not much to do. Others see it just as something they have to do to graduate, not like a service to the community. And for what my friends told me, I didn't think it was going to be different for me.

Like everyone, I went to a fair they organize every semester with different organizations that you can choose for doing your social service. They are always the same. But this time, there was one that made me instantly enroll. One where I could use what I knew from my business major to help people and create a positive impact.

They told us everything on the first meeting: Mexico is full of women entrepreneurs. Actually, for every 10 men who open a business, there are 8 women also doing it. And they found out that a company with a feminine leadership has 14% less possibility of failure.

The place that I chose had contacted, thanks to a partnership with a government office, women who were starting a business in my city and that were asking for some kind of help to grow. It turns out 88% of companies in Mexico, are managed without professional help. So that was our job in this social service. Even as students, we became mentors and business consultants to help these women entrepreneurs with their small businesses.

That's how I met Mrs Chelito. She wasn't from Silicon Valley, or on the Forbes list on Mexico's most influential women. And you won't find interviews about her experience, or her success story online. That's why I loved to meet her in person. And help her.

At more than 60 years old, Mrs Chelito realized, without any market study, but with a great intuition, that there were no close pharmacies or accessible medicine where she lived. At her age and without knowing about management or how to start a business, she came into the entrepreneurial world and opened her own pharmacy.

Since I met her, I knew she was one of those people with a smile always on their face, anytime. I bet she's a great grandma. You can see it. Every time I got there, she was excited and full of energy to improve her work. I remember she cheered herself. Maybe we should all do that to have the same energy, passion and optimism she has.

Chelito's pharmacy isn't huge or has different aisles like the big pharmacies from national chains. But it's clean and organized. And she always tries to sell the medicine at the best price. Her customers know they can trust her she's offering the best quality generic products.

The first time I saw her, we had a small interview with her and one of her employees to make a diagnosis on the business and look for ways I could help. One of the things that impressed me, was that she already had a computer to manage the inventories automatically. She told me she got it thanks to a micro credit government program. That's making the most out of opportunities!

But, like in many small companies, even with a software for inventories, finances were a little out of control. And processes were not established.

When we finished that first diagnose interview, I saw they opened a very national famous pharmacy just in front of hers.

It's unfair, because Mrs. Chelito was the first to get there, with a lot of hard work and dedication behind. And while she risked most of her money to set up her pharmacy, the one in front, being a national company, didn't have any problem getting there. I felt I was in a case like the Oxxo or 7 Eleven vs local convenience stores.

To compete with that pharmacy in front, we needed to work a lot more.

In my classes, I always solved theoretic problems from multinational companies. It was even easy to come up with solutions, even if they were complicated.

And now that I had a problem from a local business, I

didn't even know where to start.

In my head, there was the idea that anyone who knew Mrs. Chelito's story, would stop buying from other places and would become her client. Who wouldn't want to support her?

That's the problem. Every time we hear less stories from the people we have around us. And the stories we hear the most are from brands and companies that can pay a lot of money for any kind of ads.

But something special happens with the local brands.

When you know the people or the families behind a small business, and after they tell you what they have done to get there, and they talk to you about their reason for being there with such passion, something amazing happens: there is a bond. And that bond we have with local companies, should be the strongest one and the hardest to break.

I can't believe I'm saying this. On one hand, I wish we had more trade deals and less barriers to get into other countries. But I also know that making our own internal market stronger is something we have to do to make our own economy grow.

Because there's a big problem when we talk about opening businesses. It turns out that, in Mexico, from every one hundred companies that open, seventy-seven would be closing by the first year. 77! That says a lot about the way Mexicans are trying to make things and the support we give to each other.

Mrs. Chelito already went through those first years. She's part of the businesses that have made it. She opened 3 more branches with a lot of effort. There's still the topic about home delivery. Sometimes she does the deliveries herself. And she has a hard time getting doctors to work at her pharmacy to offer consultations.

But like she says: "Here we go, step by step".

And I loved to be part of them.

RESILIENCE

"Do all the good you can. In all the ways you can.
To all the people you can. As long as ever you can."

-

John Wesley (and Hillary Clinton)

Our Place

The closer I got to graduation day, the more I thought about my future and my place in the world. What was I going to do one day after my graduation and then for life? Like many, my dream is to do what I really like and I'm super passionate about. And along the way, I was going to leave my footprint in the world. There's where everything gets complicated. How do I find something that I like to do, has a good purpose, and is also well paid?

The old life model was to pick a road that would give you stability. Once you got there, you could choose a hobby that makes you happy and you could even look for a cause or someone to support. There are studies that show millennials are very different. When we look for a job or start a project, we pay more attention on how it's going to have an impact in the world. More than the money to stability it will bring, we care more about the sense and purpose of it, and how passionate we are about it.

I know, there are thousands of magazines and articles that say millennials, specially the younger ones, don't know how to do anything, don't know how to commit, will always be broke, because we don't know how to save, that we get depressed and offended by anything, that we don't take feedback, that we're lazy and we can't spend more than an hour sitting in an office. And besides all of that, that we have an addiction to using our phones. But those articles don't mention that we're focused not just on solving our own problems. Instead of just thinking about our own growth and development, we want to achieve that at the same time we help others get there. And we are focused on going a social good that impacts the world the best way possible.

It's just hard sometimes to find that job or project where you can use all your potential while you help others do the same.

It's no one's fault, not of a politician, teacher or relative, that we don't know where and how can we make that change happen. And thinking about solving all the country's problems can be exhausting. Sometimes when I think about what the biggest problem is, and when I think I have the perfect solution, I realize there are more problems or more important causes that don't seem to end. Like the lack of education, the huge amount of people in poverty, the high corruption indexes, the insecurity, and the long list of problems Mexico has.

Which one has to be solved first?

Answering that is like answering what was first, the egg or the chicken.

But what can't happen is that no one tries to solve those problems. And now that I was about to graduate, even though I didn't know what my future looked like, I was sure about something: I'm always going to be one of this who try to make things better.

I know it's going to be hard. And that sometimes it's going to look like we don't make any progress and things will be bad. But I can never forget that any effort, big or small, is worth it if you do the right thing. And I'm not alone. I know there are thousands and millions of people willing to do the right thing.

We have a challenge: The good ones, the majority, are very divided. And part of the problem why we don't progress as a country is that everyone is working on their own. And that's what we need to change. We have to find a way to work together on the things we're passionate about. That's how the world has progressed all the time. No one is going to solve everything alone.

There's a movie that makes me think about this. It's called Tomorrowland, from Disney. It came to the theaters in 2015, and even though it was a failure in tickets, I think anyone can judge it by themselves. I like the cinematography. But I think they can improve the script and in some parts I get the feeling the movie isn't well done. What I loved about it were two things: the style and the message they send in the end.

The style is like retro-futuristic. Actually, one of the first scenes is at an invention fair which thousands of people with ideas and revolutionary objects in what looks like the sixties. And in the first dialogues, I identified with Casey, the main character.

It's hard to describe ourselves. Specially, when you have an idea about what you are and you start to feel the others see you in a different way than you thought. But in the movie, Casey explained who she was in a short way "I'm an optimist", she said in one of her first lines. And the first thing that came to my mind, was: so am I. Now on my Twitter profile I wrote "I'm an optimist". And I love to be one.

But one of the big lessons I learned in my life is that not everyone has to be one. It's just one type of personality in the world. For example, before I would have loved to be part of a team where everyone was optimistic. How wrong I was. Now I see it clearly. The more diverse a group is, the better results you get. And it works with everything: creative jobs, technical and artistic ones. I love the optimists in a team, like me, but it's also important to have those who see all the possible negative scenarios, those who make numbers, who demonstrate something's not doable, who are fatalists, and those who see all the obstacles, and even those who think a project won't work, because all those opinions and ideas, make everyone find the best way to make things happen.

And there's also something important when you make teams: if people who are part of it already gave up, and don't think they can improve things, nothing they do will work. But if people from that team, even with their positive or negative attitudes, don't give up, and they are sure anything they do can have an impact, it will be the best team, because they will find together a way to make it work.

Going back to the story in the movie, Casey goes to a world in other dimension called Tomorrowland, the title of the story. And the plan the makers had for Tomorrowland was to gather humans. But not anyone, only those who didn't give up, those who still believes in a better world. And there, in that place, free from all distractions and bad things in our world, like corruption, bureaucracy, bad politics and all the problems we see daily just by going onto Twitter, they would gather to fix those bad things in the world.

It's a strong and powerful idea. Imagine there was a place like that in real life free of distractions where only the people who want to change the world go, and all the ideas and actions would come from. It would be like a place only for the people who believe we can have the Mexico we all want. And even better, only for those who want to do something.

That place would be full of people like you and me. It would be the place where I would love to be and where thousands of people would develop their potential while they help others do it and they help the world be a better place.

Because let's be honest, the government can't do it alone. We should forget about that idea that only politicians are the ones who will solve everything. The normal citizens have to get involved. There's no other way.

I liked when, the now president, Andrés Manuel López Obrador, said in his campaign that he couldn't do it alone, and that's why in his first TV ad, he asked that besides voting for him, people would vote for his party's candidates who were trying to get to Congress. Even though the campaign is over, I wish he still had the same speech saying that he can't do it alone, but now, instead of asking to vote for his party, I wish he motivated the country to be involved in one of the many causes and problems we have, and that he insisted that the citizens are the ones who have to be organized to make the changes we want.

There's a new international organization called The Good Country, and with help of many databases and research they built a ranking where they measure countries in a different way, not by GDP or the size of their economies, but for their capacity to create a common good for humanity. I loved the concept, because even though the other measurements can tell you a lot about a country, they don't tell you what they are doing to improve humanity. In this ranking, Mexico is in the 74th place. They measure things like Science and Technology, where we rank 95th, The Planet and the World, ranked 90th, and Prosperity and Equality, ranked 108th. I think we are better than those numbers. And that if we decided to solve the problems about those topics, we could easily take the first places on the ranking of the countries who do a greater good.

But the problem, sums up in the quote the same association has on their website:

> *"Most of the problems in the world are only symptoms of a bigger problem: we still haven't found the way to organize as a single species who lives in one single planet".*

And just like we can't organize as species, Mexicans haven't been able to organize as people from a single country. And that's what is missing in Mexico, and in any country where they want a change: people who organize.

As former president, Barack Obama gave a speech to Howard University graduates about what someone needs to reach their goals and the way to not leave them as dreams. With all the experience he has, he also talked about how citizens can solve problems a country or community has:

"Change requires more than anger.
Change requires a plan, it requires
organization and it requires a strategy".

This is one of the quotes from the speech that made me think the most. And one of my favorites. When we see something is wrong, we just stay on the first stage, at anger. We start to blame and we think on the long list of people who should do something to solve it. And when the extraordinary happens, and that person already wants to do something to change it, they don't know how.

When I thought Obama's speech was good enough, he added more:

"You have to go through life with
something more than just passion for
change: you have to have a strategy, not
just awareness, but action".

And it's not just words his team or communications

advisor told him to say. On the contrary. He's one of the best examples of coherence we can find.

Some years ago, after having one of the best campaigns and after he won the election for president, he launched a program called Organizing for Action. He promised he would do everything in his hands to defend and fight for the causes he believed in and the millions of people who supported him to get in the White House, but because he couldn't do it alone, he launched that organization where citizens, common people, would organize, make a plan and create a strategy to make all those changes they believed in. Obama told them: it wouldn't be easy. They would need thousands of people for getting involved to make calls to their representatives in Congress, thousands of citizens writing and sending letters, people making campaigns on social media, knocking doors and walking on the streets.

Every time I see Organizing for Action's website, I see pictures and videos from entire communities talking about problems together and finding solutions. And there's everything in those meetings: young people, kids, women, students and businessmen, everyone participating on solving the issues they have in their neighborhood or district. They take it seriously. That's why the changes they have made are big and serious. And they are doing what should be normal in any democracy: get together, give opinions, and make the representatives do what their people ask them to do.

In the end, they created movements so big that they passed laws, reforms, government programs, and everything thanks to an organized community that the former president promoted.

And he hasn't given up. Before getting out of the White House he announced he already had plans for his retirement: creating the Obama Foundation.

"Our mission is to inspire, empower and connect people to change their world. We will equip civic innovators, young leaders and common citizens with abilities and tools they need to create a change in their communities".

When he has to explain it in a few words, he talks about his foundation as a democracy school. He will keep teaching the citizens, how to make the changes we so want.

He's convinced that one action, like going to a march or signing a petition isn't going to do anything if there's not a full strategy behind. And that if we want to make a change for the long term, we need joint actions backed up by a real plan. That perspective, very realistic, that Obama has about how to make a change, inspires me. And it makes me wonder: why, doing what he says, hasn't become normal?

One of the places where people who don't give up gather, is at NGOs or civil associations. There are many around the world and about many different topics.

The organization Tech For Good made an article with data related to the topic about NGOs. They are about ten million in the world. Only in the US, there are 1.4 million NGOs. Mexico barely gets to ten thousand. They are very few for all the problems we have.

In some studies, they have tried to prove that the more people participate in a social cause or in an organization, the higher the democracy level, and the higher the wellbeing they achieve. Just to give an example, in France 44% of people actively participate in organizations that have a local cause. Who doesn't want the quality of life that country has achieved?

In The Good Country ranking I mentioned before, Mexico ranks 45th in Health and Wellbeing, and that is the topic where we do the best. When I discovered that 66% of NGOs in Mexico give access to health services, I understood the great impact ONGs can have. It's no coincidence that our best ranked topic in The Good Country is the one where more NGOs work in, the topic where most people don't give up, and are working together.

Now we know their efforts worked. The numbers that prove it are there, and those that show us the change we have to make to improve the country.

Participating in an association, or NGO, should be easier than ever before. We have many tools that can help us organize better, like all the online collaboration platforms. And now anyone with a phone can make news or an unfair situation go viral. We have to take advantage of that. Now that you can raise your voice with a simple click.

If you're still a student, you can start at a university. In the end, there are many ways of thinking. Start with your career. Imagine all it can do to improve the country. You will be surprised by the possibilities. And there are no exceptions. We need people from everywhere united. And you just need a first meeting with your neighbors to come to an agreement, list the problems the neighborhood has and start looking how they can be solved, who can you talk to, or who and how can you demand something. Or if you're one of those who want to go to the next level, what would be better than opening your own organization about the topic you are most passionate about.

This is what you need to know about NGOs and foundations: most of them work with donations. In 2015, they found that one of three people in the world, donated to a social cause. And one out of four, registered as a volunteer. They are good numbers. You see how you won't be alone if you start an organization to work for something you love?

There's another option. Also, in the book "Create or Die", I heard for the first time about a "social company" and I knew the story about Muhammad Yunus. He won the Nobel Peace Prize after creating a company that gives credits to people who are poor enough not to qualify for a regular bank credit. Everyone told him not to do it. They told him he wasn't going to get his money back and that he would lose the investment. But it was the opposite.

The Norwegian Committee of the Nobel, who decide who they give the prize, said that peace can't be achieved if big groups of people don't try to look the way to get out of poverty. That's why they gave the Nobel to Muhammad.

Because through those small credits he created an economic and social development from below. And it's not through a foundation based on donations. It's through a social company called Grameen Bank.

When Andrés Oppenheimer interviewed him, he first explained how capitalism went the wrong way when it stopped solving social problems. And then he says that businessmen, for example, instead of making donations, "should create, besides their companies for profit, social companies, that are self-sufficient and more sustainable than NGOs who depend from charity".

The main difference between an ONG and a social company is the way they operate and get resources. A social company solves a problem and has a positive impact on society, but is also a good business. Like any other company, it will probably need investment at the beginning. And it's not wrong to get that investment back while the profits go to everything needed to fulfill the purpose and mission of the company.

That's not profiting on problems. It's all the opposite. Is solving them. And having a totally self-sufficient, sustainable, and profitable structure so you can keep doing it the best way.

In the US there's a different electoral system than ours. The one who gets more votes not always wins, like in the 2016 election where Hillary Clinton got most of the votes, with almost a three million votes more than Donald Trump, but she didn't win the electoral votes form the states. It's weird to think that, even though most people vote for a candidate, it doesn't mean they will win.

Even though I don't live there, I was always looking at the election and many others in the world (hi Macron!). In the end, what happens in the world affects us and the decisions their leaders make in topics like international trade or migration. Now we can see it with the endless fight about who will pay for Trump's wall on the border with Mexico, the tariffs for Mexican products, like steel, and the leak of foreign investment that was scheduled to get to our country. And let's not talk about the new taxes for the US companies who want to produce here and not there, the separation and how they treat migrant families at the border, and all the stamping Trump has given us, even in our own territory.

On November 8, 2016, three days after my birthday, I was at a work dinner. The mayor had awarded some outstanding young people from the city, and we invited them for dinner. And the talk was centered in one thing only: who was going to win the elections in the US? That day, people had already voted and the results were coming out.

Every five minutes, we all looked at our phones waiting or some news.

The New York Times published some days before, that there was 98% chance Hillary Clinton would win, according to all the surveys and statistics they had. And it wasn't only them. It was weird to see a forecast where she didn't win. Because of that, and because I thought she did one of the best campaigns in history, when Trump started to upload the count of electoral votes, I started telling everyone at the dinner, and also my friends in WhatsApp, that we shouldn't worry. The results that were coming out were the ones from red states, the republican ones.

I stayed up all night waiting for the final results. There I was, sitting in the kitchen, at 2 in the morning, with my computer with thousands of tabs open from different news websites, and talking to two of my best friends who were doing the same.

And I was still sure Hillary was going to win. Until the math no longer added up, and the news declared Donald

Trump as the winner, who came out to accept victory with a totally improvised speech.

The next day in my negotiation classes. I was wearing black. Maybe now it sounds like too much, but that day, in Twitter and all the news, I saw a lot of videos and posts of kids crying because they were afraid, Muslims who didn't know if they could go out, Mexican migrants without understanding what would happen from now on, and in general, everyone in shock because a candidate with a hate and division speech had won the presidency.

No one knew what happened.

And many things would change since then.

Many complained to the Mexican government that they had made Trump win because they invited him like if they were receiving a head of state even when he was still in campaign.

And worse, after he had already insulted Mexicans in several speeches.

It was until April 2018, two years later, that Enrique Peña Nieto sent a strong and clear message to the stamping Trump had been giving us:

"There is something that unites and
summons everyone, and absolutely all
Mexicans: the certainty that nothing, nor
anyone, is above the dignity of Mexico".

It was the first time in his government that I felt proud about what he said.

We were in campaign, and the five candidates for president backed him up. And the entire country too. My Facebook and Twitter were full of posts of friends and people sharing the same message.

That's what a president does: unite us.

But in the US, like we can see it daily, the president does the opposite. Since he started his campaign, Trump bet on division and fear. And his government has been like that too. We don't have to look a lot. It's enough to see how in his first days he signed an executive order to block the entrance for Muslims, how he started separating migrant families and locking kids in cages and how he makes those kids be their own lawyers at trials.

But there, like in many other countries, they have been practicing the route that says that, if you're not part of the solution, you are part of the problem.

Trump won. He will promote his ideas and agenda as

much as he can. That's why his voters picked him, and that's how a democracy works. But because of that, we need counterweights. And that counterweight is stronger than ever.

After the shock was over, the sadness, denial, desperation, and anger, incredible NGOs were born, about different topics and each one of them with very different objectives.

Among my favorites is Run for Something. I love it so much I always talk about it. This organization promotes and recruits progressive millennials to look for a public office. Amanda Litman, the co-founder and director, was part of Hillary Clinton's campaign in 2016. You can imagine the disappointment she felt when they lost. But she made that turn into a project that is changing her country's history. Some months after, while president Trump was being sworn in, on January 21st, 2017, she was publishing a website about her new organization and announcing it everywhere in social media. In some interviews she said she didn't think it was going to be so successful. Her goal was to register a hundred people interested in running for public office. They have more than ten thousand.

Running for office is a huge task. Mostly, for the one who is their first time. And it's also a lot of responsibility. That organization chooses first the profiles they will support so they are the best and that every time the citizens see a candidate is backed up by them it will be a warranty. And they don't leave them alone. They are with them along the way. They train them and give them any kind of coaching. From making their proposals to how to raise money and create a base of citizen support. Even win.

Just one year after, 50% of the candidates they backed up won. I can't imagine what they will do in the long term. Who knows. Maybe they even back someone up for president and they will win.

Just like Run for Something, there are many more. Most of them with people from my generation in charge.

Latino Victory to grow Latin power in government, and Us politics. The Arena, to train and coach in civic responsibility. Indivisible, to combat Trump's divisive agenda. Color of Change, to make racial justice. And the list goes on. In Twitter I follow all of them. And their founders They give me my daily motivation and energy shot. Even though it's not our country, they give me confidence that young people are the ones who will fix things in the world. And that's about to happen in Mexico too.

Another example is David Hogg, the high school student who survived one of the terrible shootings in Florida. Now he's one of the biggest activists with the movement "Never Again". Their goal is to pass a bill about gun control. I couldn't imagine what it would feel to be in one of my classes, and see someone go in with a gun. And that they start shooting my classmates. David got to turn sadness and the desperation he felt, into a movement. Now he's making history. And Mexicans can also write ours.

Let's take these examples. They are just in front of us. And they are working. Supporting the leaderships of different causes is very important. We have to start uniting. Not to divide ourselves.

Let's promote that participating making a change, with politics, ONGs or any other activity, is seen as something honorable and positive. Thinking the opposite made us get away from that, when it needs to be the other way. Participating in this should be like a second job or an extracurricular activity for everyone. Because it affects us all!

I hope one day I can see news about new Mexican

organizations that are changing Mexico's history. With young people in front. Convinced that any small action can change the way we're going.

"Faith in action is love.
And love in action is service"

–

Mother Teresa

No One Else But You

In high school, one day, the principal asked for me to talk for a while in his office. After we said hi and asking me how everything was going, he stood up, walked to his bookcase and got a black book out. It was the biography of the US presidents and some of Mexico's presidents. He was looking through it without saying anything until he found what he was looking for. And he started reading me the story of Abraham Lincoln.

At 22, he had already failed in business and was completely bankrupt. Because he's passionate about solving problems in his country he ran for public office, but he lost. Then, he ran again, but he lost again. In total, he tried nine times, without success. His girlfriend, that she was going to marry, died. And after more difficult situations, the tenth time he ran for public office, he won. And that election he won, was the presidency. And what he achieved from there, was history.

In that moment, I was going through my own failure at sixteen. And the message the principal tried to give me with Lincoln's story was clear: we can only try, try, and try again. There's no other way to get what we want than to work, until what seems impossible, becomes possible.

It's not just Lincoln's story among those who were successful after surviving great failures. There you have Oprah Winfrey when she was fired for not being a good Tv host in her first job. And Steven Spielberg being rejected two times by USC Cinematic Arts, Walt Disney, when he was young, also being fired for lack of imagination and good ideas, J.K. Rowling being rejected by twelve editorials before one agreed to publish her book, and Steve Jobs being fired from his own company.

We listen and listen to stories, but it seems like none, nor all of them together, are enough to take away the paradigm that failure is bad. We're still afraid of it. And fear to fail, and to what people will say, is what stops millions of people from acting and reaching their dreams.

It's normal. Feeling fear is one of the instincts we have by nature. For thousands of years the human being has survived, in part, for recognizing danger situations. By instinct we try to avoid the situations where we feel insecure. But there are rational fears, like the fear to fall from a cliff, and fears that stop us, like the fear of things not going the way we thought.

But we have to remember this: we won't always control everything that happens to us. The only thing we can control is how we react to everything that happens. And want it or not, we will all deal with failures and disappointments. That's why it's important to do everything to be resilient, I mean, to wake up and recover no matter what.

This is the second time I quote Eleanor Roosevelt, but now with something she said about how to recover from failure and disappointment:

> *"You get strength, courage, and*
> *confidence with every experience where*
> *you stop and see fears in the eye and you*
> *are able to tell yourself: 'I lived this horror,*
> *I can take whatever is next'".*

And it's important to remember, because when

something bad happens in our lives, we think we are the only ones having a hard time and we feel we won't recover ever. But we can overcome everything.

In the movie "The Iron Lady", besides Meryl Streep's amazing acting, there's a quote Margaret Thatcher says just when she got elected as the first woman ever to become Prime Minister in the history of the UK:

> *"Take care of your thoughts because they will become your words. Take care of your words, because they will become your actions. Take care of your actions, because they will become your habits. And take care of your habits, because they will become your destiny".*

This quote has been with me since then, because it reminds me the important a simple thought can be and what can it become. And now, I like to be careful with what I think and listen. Because everything that you have around you will influence how you think, and as a result, who you are. So, it's important to ask yourself: Who do you listen to every day and what do you talk about? In your talks, do they cheer and motivate you or they take energy away from you and make you feel you can't do something? What kind of movies you watch and what do you read about? What songs you like and what are they about? And who do you follow on Instagram and Twitter?

If I was always listening to people who complain about everything, people who only see the bad side of life, and people who don't want to serve others, not even me could stay positive. But I try to surround myself with people who are the opposite, I take care of the music I listen to, the videos I watch, and the books I read.

In Tomorrowland they repeat a lot a little tale I love to remember:

> *There are two wolves inside of us. And they are always fighting. One is darkness and desperation. The other one is light and hope. Which one of the wolves wins the fight? The one you feed.*

It's also really important to ask yourself: who are your role models?

I have my own list of people I admire. Maybe with this book you can have an idea of who they are. I like to listen to their speeches and look at what they do. All of them have something in common: they keep going despite the failures they had, they keep challenging themselves, and they help others do it. Actually, every time I feel without energy, or when I don't feel motivated, I like to think about what they would do in my place. Sometimes I imagine they are with me to cheer me up and remind me life is about trying, trying, and trying again and again.

This doesn't mean I'm not realistic. I also like to see the news about what is happening in the world. Sometimes it's discouraging. And sometimes it looks like the problems my country and the world have will never get fixed. Just like you, I saw things that make me think we won't have the Mexico we all want. But Denisse Dresser wrote:

> *"In front of all the motives to close the eyes, there are all the motives to open them. In front of all the reasons to lose faith in Mexico, there are all the reasons to recover it".*

I'm never going to forget the picture of the dead kid by the shore in Syria that went viral in 2015. It was a reminder that the world isn't ok.

Still in the twenty-first century, there are places where human rights aren't respected, there's war, gender inequality, hunger, poverty, and many more problems that are only growing, instead of getting smaller, like pollution and migration crisis.

It is what it is. It's the world we inherited. And we have two choices: not to worry, don't do anything, and leave it like that. Or start acting and building the world like we think it should be.

If you're convinced, like me, that we have to start building the world as we think it should be, we have to hurry. Can you imagine when future generations look back and see what went on? I'm sure they will ask how we let so many unfairnesses happen and didn't do anything about it.

There's a movie about the scientist who invented Zyklon B. The purpose was to create a product to clean and disinfect surfaces. But it ended up being used to kill a million people in the gas chambers in Auschwitz. When the scientist realized what the Nazis were using his invention for, he tried to talk to his friends, the church, and any authority in his country to try to stop what was happening at the concentration camps. No one believed him, or no one wanted to believe him. Now we know they didn't stop. And that no one did anything.

When I was in those same concentration camps in Auschwitz, I asked myself many times why humanity, at that time, didn't stop what was happening. There was still no UN, and maybe communication was slower than now. But anyone with a little bit of compassion and decency would have noticed they were in front of a mortal and humanitarian crisis.

We can make the same question now. What are we doing to stop the injustices from this time?

This is one of my favorite tweets lately:

> *"The Holocaust was legal and the people who gave shelter to Jews were criminals. Slavery was legal and people who freed slaves were criminals. Segregation between black and white was legal and anyone who fought or defended equality was a criminal. So, the government and the laws should not be a guide for decency or human morality".*

We're stepping on giants' shoulders who fought against the injustices of their time so today we can have all the liberties and rights we have. And we can't stop. It's like a relay race. We all have to take the baton and keep going.

There's interesting data in a study made by Western Union. They interviewed, in 2017, more than ten thousand young people who were between twenty and thirty-six years old. Basically, they interviewed millennials. Among the answers they got, this was my favorite: almost nine out of every ten said they wanted to participate or at least give their opinion on future global and national topics. If it's like that, we're already good. Because it's true that we need everyone's ideas to start solving the current problems the world has and start acting to stop injustices. And I feel proud that most people from my generation has something to say and do in the search for solutions.

But something doesn't add up. Because it's been proved that millennials are between the age range of people who vote the least in an election. And not only in Mexico. It happens all over the world. We don't take advantage of the fact that young people are more than half of the population, and that we can decide, literally, the way our city, state, and country are going, just by going to vote.

Some days before the midterm elections in the US, by the end of 2018, Barack Obama posted a video with all the excuses we sometimes hear from people who are doubting if they should vote or no. In the middle of the video, he said: Would you let your grandma pick the playlist for your parties?". He said it as a joke, but his message is true. If we wouldn't let anyone else choose our playlist, something so simple in our lives, why do we let others make the decisions about the county's future?

Other results from that same Western Union study were worrying. Like the fact that eight out of ten young people though the world is more divided now than it was in 2015. And more than half thinks it will be even more divided by 203. We just have to look at what's happening in the whole world. In the US a candidate who was against minorities and in campaign was always talking badly about them won. In Scotland, the referendum to keep being part of the UK won by very little. In the UK, they voted to get out of the European Union. And in the rest of the world there seems to be a speech of hatred, division and paranoia getting bigger and bigger.

We don't have to go that far. In Mexico we're creating division every time some insults someone else because of their beliefs or preferences. Maybe it started as a joke. But it's not anymore. Every time we accuse someone of being part of the power mafia, being fifí, peje zombie, or chairo, we're setting labels and dividing us more than we already are. Anyone would get angry by that. That's not what the country needs. It's supposed that all political ideas (in theory) promote respect and diversity. And if someone can't be with people who think differently or if they can't listen to different ideas and opinions, to start, they shouldn't have a public office or be part of a country's politics. Because diversity of ideas is what makes a democracy work.

What we need more than ever, is people who unite us to make better decisions. It's like in companies. Sometimes there are bosses that only want to divide their own team and take only their own opinion into account and never listen anyone else. But there are also the leaders who unite and take advantage of the potential of their teams, no one is more important, they solve problems together and they find new ways of making things quickly and efficiently.

Everyday, we can be the difference between what's promoted in our community, our social media, and our houses. There are many anger and division messages, but if all the good people, the optimists and inclusive people shared what they thought and feel, you would be surprised that it's the majority.

Something gives me hope. 90% of the interviewed millennials agreed that a better global future can be reached through collaboration between people and nations. Instead of competing against each other, we are willing to work in team to make everyone do better, not just a few.

The time to start that future is now. Just like this, collaborating. Imagine that we could be so connected to each other. And that, instead of being citizens of a country, we could be citizens of the world.

When I was in Europe, I visited Saint Stephen's cathedral in Vienna. Inside there was a large space where visitors could light up a candle, ask for something, and leave it lit. Just a few days before, the world had seen how a bus intentionally ran over those who were celebrating Bastille Day in Nice. Almost ninety people died. I lit up a candle for them and for all the people who were suffering some injustice. I left it there, took a picture, and posted it with this quote:

> "*The world needs courage, hope, faith,*
> *and perseverance*".

Some years went by and I still believe more in that quote.

I woke up on December 11th after years of waiting for that day. It was one of those times where you open your eyes before the alarm sounds because you're excited and nervous at the same time for what will happen in the day. I saw the time and I took a shower. I had my suit ready, my blue tie, and my shoes. I saved, did my hair, I wore "Seoul", my favorite lotion, and just when I had to get out, in the last minute, I switched the tie for a black one. Blue is my favorite color, but this was an important and serious day.

Before getting out of the house, I opened the black journal that has always been there in my important days. You can say I'm very sentimentalist, but a few years ago I wrote a small note for myself, just to read on that day.

> *Alfonso:*
>
> *Congratulations! After all, you did it. I know you're probably feeling and thinking a lot. And maybe you're afraid or worried about the future and everything that's next.*
>
> *But this is the most important thing you have to know today: never forget that if you want to succeed in life, you have to find a way to serve more people.*

I got in the car, put on my favorite playlist, and drove to my university for the last time. On the way, I thought about that note I wrote a few years ago.

Serving, just like being kind, is seen sometimes as a weakness. But there's no substitute for that. And I could realize even more tat men and women who serve are kinder, and are the strongest. Besides, it's what the world needs. Simply going out on the street or even opening some post's comments, you can realize all the hatred and pessimism there is in people. So, I'm glad that this is the message I left for myself in that time for now.

And the good news is that anyone can serve others. It's not so hard. And it applies to everything.

I don't usually read poems. I don't understand some of them. But I have my favorite one. Thinking about it, it's the only one I like. It's called "The pleasure of serving". And it was written by Gabriela Mistral, the first latin person to get a Nobel Literature Prize. When I knew that, I liked this poem even more:

All of nature is a yearning for service:
The cloud serves, and the wind,
and the furrow.
Where there is a tree to plant,
you be the one.

Where there is a mistake to undo,
let it be you.

You be the one to remove the rock from
the field,
The hate from human hearts,
And the difficulties from the problem.

There is joy in being wise and just,
But above all there is the beautiful,
The immense happiness of serving.

How sad the world would be if all was
already done.
If there was no rosebush to plant,
No enterprise to undertake.

Do not limit yourself to easy tasks.
It's so beautiful to do what others dodge.
But don't fall prey to the error that only.
Great tasks done can be counted as
accomplishments.

There are small acts of service that are
good ones:
Decoratively setting a table,
Putting some books in order,
Combing a little girl's hair.

That one over there is the one that
criticizes,
This other one is the one that destroys.
You be the one that serves.
Serving is not a labor just for inferior
beings.

God, who gives fruit and light, serves.
His name could be rendered thus:
He Who Serves.
And he has his eyes on our hands,
And he asks us at the close of day:
"Did you render service today? To whom?
To a tree, to your friend, to your mother?"

There will always be a lot of work to do, a lot of things
to change, and causes to fight for. If you think someone
should fix the world, there's no one better than you to do
it. That's what serving is about. The more people that do it,
the better we will all do. And you don't have to open a
foundation or make a millionaire donation to feel you're
serving. Like the example in the poem, you can serve even
with the smallest action in things that are part of your daily
life.

And now that I see everything going back, serving, was what I did during all these years as a college student.

I enrolled into a career thinking I had a lot to learn to fix the world. When I opened my own student group, called Voz Joven, I did it being sure that young people had a lot to say and a lot to do to change the country. And every event and activity we did, and every cause we promoted, we did it being aware that, if we convinced, at least someone to do the right thing, our mission would be accomplished. Later I got into my first full time job, where I had the chance to serve to make a greater good than the one I did before. In team, we achieved to make our city the second best to live in the entire country. When I went abroad, i did it with open eyes to see what those countries were doing to grow and become better, being sure that we could do the same here in Mexico. And like that, in each of my projects, and each of my plans, what always gave me energy, is thinking I can serve. And is what always will.

Now, no one can complain that I didn't try to change things. In one way or another, everything that is in this book were my attempts to make my university, my city and my country improve. And even though I got into a lot of trouble while doing it, I'm still here alive.

A little stress and hard work never killed anyone.

When I got to my university, I couldn't avoid to feel nostalgic after many years I spent there, walking on the hallways between classrooms, walking on the gardens and visiting the library. I spent entire days and nights there, literally, sometimes studying or doing homework, and sometimes planning projects I believed in with all my heart.

Seeing my university, that day, full of people that, like me, were accomplishing one more goal, made me feel even more optimistic about the future that we have to build together.

First, there was a breakfast for all the graduates. All the International Business graduates were in my table. After spending so many years together in the same classes, that was the last time we were all there together.

After, we went to the auditorium for the official graduation ceremony. I was finally there, in the moment every student dream of.

Many things happened while I got my degree. Many successes and many failures. And many lessons that will stay with me for the rest of my life, good and bad ones. But of all those lessons, all of them, were so worth it. Now I am who I am thanks to all of them. And also, thanks to those lessons, I'm more prepared than before to face anything needed to reach my goals.

I learned like crazy. And I'm grateful with all my professors who made it possible. It was also hard for them to put up with someone who always had an opinion and many things to do, besides their classes.

And even though I didn't end with the perfect GDP I would have wanted, when I took the national exam CENEVAL with all my career topics, I got Outstanding. It was like a reminder to myself that I loved and was passionate about the career I chose. And that when I set a goal, and focus, I can do it.

When they mentioned my name, I went to the front, shook the hand of people who were there, and I got my degree. Just in that moment, a very important stage in my life was close, the best until now.

In the end, I hugged my parents and my grandparents. They were all there. They were waiting for that day more than me. I was officially the first grandson to graduate college.

I took pictures with some of my favorite professors and my friends. I wasn't going to see them every day, like I used to. And now everyone would follow their own path. But that's the nice thing about knowing people: each one of them is in this world to achieve different things, in different places. If we all came to do the same, it would be very boring. And that's what makes this world so special: that we all have our own story, very different from others.

At night, after celebrating that special and important day, and when I could find time and space just for me, the question I had been asking myself for months came in again: Now what?

The answer was easy.

Keep going. Serve. Be kind. Try to do good all the time. And try to change my country and the whole world.

Now it's your turn to make
the impossible, possible.

Follow me:

Instagram @aguirrealfonso

Twitter @aguirrealfonso

Facebook.com/aguirrealfonso